FATHERS AND SONS

by the same author

THE ENEMY WITHIN (Gallery Press)

SELECTED PLAYS OF BRIAN FRIEL: PHILADELPHIA,
HERE I COME!, THE FREEDOM OF THE CITY,
LIVING QUARTERS, ARISTOCRATS, FAITH HEALER
and TRANSLATIONS

THE LOVES OF CASS McGUIRE

LOVERS

VOLUNTEERS

THE COMMUNICATION CORD

THREE SISTERS (*A Translation*) (Gallery Press)

Sept. 87

FATHERS
AND SONS

BRIAN FRIEL

after the novel by
Ivan Turgenev

_For Pat Burke, with best wishes.
Brian Friel_

faber and faber
LONDON · BOSTON

First published in 1987
by Faber and Faber Limited
3 Queen Square London WC1N 3AU

Typeset by Goodfellow & Egan, Cambridge

Printed in Great Britain by
Redwood Burn Ltd Trowbridge Wiltshire
All rights reserved

© Brian Friel, 1987

British Library Cataloguing in Publication Data

Friel, Brian
Fathers and sons.
I. Title   II. Turgenev, I.S.
822'.914   PR6056.R5

ISBN 0-571-15079-9

for Tom and Julie

CHARACTERS

ARKADY NIKOLAYEVICH KIRSANOV	Student (twenty-two)
YEVGENY VASSILYICH BAZAROV	Student (twenty-two)
NIKOLAI PETROVICH KIRSANOV	Arkady's father; estate owner (forty-four)
PAVEL PETROVICH KIRSANOV	Arkady's uncle; retired guardsman (forty-five)
VASSILY IVANYICH BAZAROV	Bazarov's father; retired army doctor (sixties)
ARINA VLASSYEVNA BAZAROV	Bazarov's mother (fifties)
FENICHKA FEDOSYA NIKOLAYEVNA	Nikolai's mistress (twenty-three)
ANNA SERGEYEVNA ODINTSOV	Estate owner; widow (twenty-nine)
KATYA SERGEYEVNA	Anna's sister (eighteen)
PRINCESS OLGA	Anna's aunt (seventies)
DUNYASHA	Servant in Kirsanov home (twenties)
PROKOFYICH	Servant in Kirsanov home (sixties)
PIOTR	Servant in Kirsanov home (nineteen)
TIMOFEICH	Servant in Bazarov home (sixties)
FEDKA	Servant in Bazarov home (sixteen)

MUSIC

ACT ONE

Scene 1 – Beethoven's *Romance* (for violin and orchestra) in F-major, Op. 50.

Scene 2 – Piano duets. In marching, military style.

ACT TWO

Scene 1 – Beethoven's *Romance* in G-major, Op. 40.

Scene 2 – As in Act One Scene 1.

Scene 3 – *Te Deum Laudamus*.

Scene 4 – 'Drink to me only' (vocal and piano).

– 'Drink to me only' (played on piano-accordion).

Fathers and Sons opened at the Lyttelton Theatre, South Bank, London, on 8 July 1987. The cast was as follows:

ARKADY NIKOLAYEVICH KIRSANOV	Ralph Fiennes
YEVGENY VASSILYICH BAZAROV	Robert Glenister
NIKOLAI PETROVICH KIRSANOV	Alec McCowen
PAVEL PETROVICH KIRSANOV	Richard Pasco
VASSILY IVANYICH BAZAROV	Robin Bailey
ARINA VLASSYEVNA BAZAROV	Barbara Jefford
FENICHKA FEDOSYA NIKOLAYEVNA	Lesley Sharp
ANNA SERGEYEVNA ODINTSOV	Meg Davies
KATYA SERGEYEVNA	Robin McCaffrey
PRINCESS OLGA	Joyce Grant
DUNYASHA	Hazel Ellerby
PROKOFYICH	Antony Brown
PIOTR	Jay Villiers
TIMOFEICH	Peter Halliday
FEDKA	Jim Millea

Directed by	Michael Rudman
Designed by	Carl Toms
Music	Matthew Scott

ACT ONE

SCENE ONE

Before the scene begins bring up the sound of Beethoven's Romance *in F-major, Op. 50, played by Nikolai on the cello. Early afternoon in May, 1859.*

The garden-lawn in front of the Kirsanov home. We can see into the living-room upstage. A veranda runs across the front of the house with two steps leading down to the garden. Some potted plants in front of the veranda. Downstage left there is a gazebo/summer-house. Various summer seats and stools. (Left and right from the point of view of the audience.) Characters enter from the left – i.e. the yard, outhouses, servants' quarters off – or from the house.

NIKOLAI *is playing the cello in the living-room.* FENICHKA *is sitting in the gazebo, knitting a garment for her baby who is sleeping in a pram at her side. She is an attractive young woman with innate dignity and confidence; but because she is no longer a servant and not yet mistress in the house she is not fully at ease in her environment. Occasionally she glances into the pram. She leaves aside her knitting, closes her eyes and sits listening to the music.*

DUNYASHA *enters left carrying a laundry-basket full of clothes. She is a plump, open-natured, open-hearted, practical-minded girl who loves to laugh.*

DUNYASHA: Oh my God, this heat has me destroyed. How do you stick it?

FENICHKA: You should have something on your head.

DUNYASHA: I met the new estate-manager over there at the clothes-line. Do you know him?

FENICHKA: Only to see.

DUNYASHA: He is just so beautiful – isn't he? I could spend my days just gazing at him, with that glossy black moustache and those sleepy brown eyes. Did you notice that beautiful black 'tash?

FENICHKA: Dunyasha!

(DUNYASHA *flops down beside her.* FENICHKA *begins knitting again.*)

DUNYASHA: Honestly. All he'd have to do is raise his little finger

I

and I'd kiss his feet. Anyhow he looked at me and he said, 'Are you going to faint, little one?' All the same that was nice, wasn't it? – 'little one'. And I said, 'What d'you mean – am I going to faint?' 'Oh,' he said, 'your face is all bloated and red.'

FENICHKA: (*Laughing*) He did not. That's another of your stories.

DUNYASHA: Cross my heart. (*Into pram.*) Hello, Mitya. How are you today, my little darling? Are you well? (*She spreads out under the sun.*) Beautiful. This must be the hottest May ever. (*Eyes closed.*) Is that the big fiddle he's playing?

FENICHKA: You know very well it's called a cello.

DUNYASHA: Sort of nice, isn't it? Bit lonely – like himself.

FENICHKA: Is he lonely?

DUNYASHA: You should know. Not much good for dancing.

FENICHKA: I heard you were dancing last night.

DUNYASHA: Five this morning. Oh, that heat's lovely.

FENICHKA: Any good?

DUNYASHA: You mean did I click? (*She sits up.*) Tell me this, Fenichka: remember all those young fellows used to be at the dances when you and I went together – all that laughing and all that fun – remember?

FENICHKA: Yes.

DUNYASHA: Well, where in God's name have they gone to, those boys? Or haven't they young brothers? All you see now are half-drunk louts that say things like, 'My God, girl, but you're a powerful armful of meat.'

(FENICHKA *laughs*.)

It's true. That's what a big clodhopper said to me last night. And if it's not the clodhoppers it's the usual old lechers with their eyes half-closed and their hands groping your bum. (*She sees* PAVEL *entering left with a book under his arm. She gets quickly to her feet.* PAVEL *is the typical 'Europeanized' Russian of the nineteenth century – wears English clothes, speaks French. His manner is jaded but his emotions function fully and astutely.*)

Jesus, here comes the Tailor's Dummy! He must have spotted you.

2

FENICHKA: Don't go, Dunyasha. Stay with me.

DUNYASHA: You're well fit to handle that old goat. And Dunyasha's place is in the kitchen.

FENICHKA: Please.

DUNYASHA: You're too gentle. Tell him straight out to bugger off.
(*She rises, makes a curtsy to* PAVEL *and exits quickly left, leaving her basket behind her.*
The relationship between PAVEL *and* FENICHKA *is uneasy.*
He looks into the pram and then at FENICHKA.)

PAVEL: Am I intruding?

FENICHKA: No. Not at all.

PAVEL: Will you be sending into town for groceries today?

FENICHKA: Yes.

PAVEL: Would you order something for me?

FENICHKA: What do you want?

PAVEL: Tea. Green tea. If you would.

FENICHKA: Of course.

PAVEL: Half a pound would suffice.

FENICHKA: I'll see to that.

PAVEL: *Merci bien.* (*Into pram.*) Hello-hello-hello-hello. He has very strong fingers. Maybe he'll be a cellist like his father. How do you like your new bedroom, Fenichka?

FENICHKA: I love it. It gets the sun in the early morning.

PAVEL: I see your light on very often in the middle of the night.
(*She rises and gathers her things.*)

FENICHKA: That's his lordship – cutting a new tooth. Aren't you cutting a new tooth, you rascal, and keeping your mother awake at night?

PAVEL: Tu es très belle.

FENICHKA: Sorry?

PAVEL: Look – he won't let me go.

FENICHKA: Let your uncle go, Mitya.

PAVEL: Fenichka—

FENICHKA: I think I'll take him inside. This sun's a bit hot for him.

PAVEL: All I want to say is—
(*He gets no further because* PROKOFYICH *enters left. He is an elderly retainer, excessively dignified and formal in manner; but*

now he is so excited, indeed so confused, that he almost runs across the stage and proclaims too loudly to nobody in particular:)

PROKOFYICH: The carriage has arrived! He's back! Master Arkady is back!

PAVEL: That's early. They must have made good time.

PROKOFYICH: The carriage is here! He has arrived! He has arrived!

PAVEL: A bit of life about the place.

FENICHKA: Yes.

PAVEL: Fenichka, forgive me if—

PROKOFYICH: Master Arkady is back! The carriage is here! Arkady's home from Petersburg!

(PROKOFYICH *is now on the veranda and calling into the living-room.* NIKOLAI *emerges with the cello-bow in his hand. He walks with a slight limp. He is a kind, decent, generous-spirited man, vague and bumbling at times but always fully alert to what is happening around him.*)

The carriage is here! Arkady's home! He's back! He's back!

PAVEL: All right, Prokofyich, we hear you.

NIKOLAI: Did you hear the news?

PAVEL: I think so, Nikolai.

NIKOLAI: Arkady has arrived from Petersburg. Wonderful! Where's Piotr? Piotr! Somebody help him with the luggage. Go and meet him, Pavel. (*To* FENICHKA.) He'll probably want something to eat, won't he? Everything's in such confusion. This is no welcome. Piotr! I'm really going to have to reprimand that young scamp.

(*General confusion and excitement.* PROKOFYICH *rushes off left.* DUNYASHA *rushes on and picks up her basket.*)

DUNYASHA: (*Privately to* FENICHKA) He has a friend with him! Get out your smelling-salts! O sweet Saviour!

FENICHKA: Take the pram inside, Dunyasha, will you?

DUNYASHA: Wait till you see *him*! A dark god! Jesus, could this be my lucky day?!

PAVEL: Who is he bringing with him, Nikolai?

NIKOLAI: Dunyasha, tell Piotr I want him – immediately!

(*She dashes off with the pram and basket.*)

4

Yes, he's bringing a friend with him – a young man called –
called – I'm sorry, I've forgotten, Pavel. I'm really going to
sack that boy.

(ARKADY *enters*.)

Ah! There he is! Arkady! Arkady!

ARKADY: Father! How are you!

(*Father and son embrace with great warmth. Already* ARKADY
is beginning to resemble his father. PROKOFYICH, *cases in his
hands, stands in the background and beams*.)

NIKOLAI: Welcome home! Welcome home, graduate!

ARKADY: Thank you.

NIKOLAI: Let me look at you. You're different. Have you lost
weight? You're altogether different. Have you eaten? You're
pale – that's it – you're very pale—

ARKADY: All that study and all those exams. What I need is a
long rest. Uncle Pavel!

PAVEL: Welcome back, Arkady.

ARKADY: It's great to see you.

(*They embrace warmly*.)

And . . . Fenichka. It *is* Fenichka, isn't it?

FENICHKA: It is.

NIKOLAI: Of course it is.

ARKADY: Indeed. Good to see you, Fenichka.

FENICHKA: And you, Arkady.

(*They shake hands and she leaves*.)

NIKOLAI: Prokofyich usually drives so slowly, we didn't expect
you until much later. Had you a good journey?

ARKADY: It was all right. I've brought a friend with me, Father.

NIKOLAI: You mentioned that in your last letter. Great.

ARKADY: His name is Bazarov.

NIKOLAI: Wonderful. We'll have a full house again. And wait till
you see your bedroom – we've had it all repapered. Pavel
chose the colour scheme.

PAVEL: That was a major row.

NIKOLAI: No, it wasn't – was it?

PAVEL: A minor row.

ARKADY: His name is Bazarov – Yevgeny Vassilyich Bazarov. I
would like you to make him very welcome.

5

NIKOLAI: Naturally we'll make him very welcome. Won't we, Pavel?

ARKADY: Our friendship is very important to me.

PAVEL: Did he graduate, too?

ARKADY: Next year. He's doing natural science and medicine. He's probably the most brilliant man I've ever met.

NIKOLAI: Well, the brilliant Bazarov is every bit as welcome as you are . . . well, almost.

ARKADY: Would you go and meet him, Uncle Pavel?

PAVEL: (To ARKADY) See? Still the message-boy. *Plus ça change* . . .

(PAVEL *goes off and* PROKOFYICH *is about to follow him.*)

NIKOLAI: And isn't Prokofyich looking well?

ARKADY: Prokofyich never changes. Thank you for picking us up.

PROKOFYICH: My pleasure. We'll go out looking for birds' nests tomorrow morning.

ARKADY: First thing. We'll show Bazarov all the good spots.

PROKOFYICH: Maybe you and I should go by ourselves first and then we—

PAVEL: (*Off*) Prokofyich!

PROKOFYICH: Coming, sir. (*To* ARKADY.) It's good to have you back, Arkady.

ARKADY: Thank you.

(PROKOFYICH *exits left.*)

Bird-nesting! He thinks I'm still a schoolboy.

NIKOLAI: In a way so do I.

ARKADY: And I deliberately mentioned Bazarov because they didn't get on very well on the journey. Prokofyich prefers the old ways, the old formalities. (*Embraces the father again.*) It's great to see you, Father.

NIKOLAI: Thank you.

ARKADY: And you're looking very fresh.

NIKOLAI: Fresh? At my age?

ARKADY: And so is Uncle Pavel. What's he doing with himself these days?

NIKOLAI: Oh, you know Pavel – killing time, as he says himself – walking – reading – (*Whispers.*) going to his English tailor

6

and his French barber – thinking his own very secret thoughts . . . (*After a quick look round.*) Arkady, there's one little matter before the others join us – I'm really a bit embarrassed mentioning it—

ARKADY: It's about Fenichka.

NIKOLAI: Shhh. How did you know?

ARKADY: Intuition.

NIKOLAI: Yes, it's about Fenichka. You know Fenichka, don't you? What am I talking about – of course you do! Well, as you know, Arkady, I've been very fond of her for a long time now. Her mother was the best housekeeper we ever had here and Fenichka has taken on those responsibilities with great assurance and skill, considering she's only twenty-three, just a year older than yourself; so I'm old enough to be her father, too, amn't I? Ha-ha. Anyhow, as I say, I've been very attached to her for a long time now; and indeed I have asked her – I have insisted – that she move out of that damp flat above the laundry and come into the main house. And I mention this now, Arkady, partly because I – I – because she's afraid you might . . . well, disapprove of her.

ARKADY: I might disapprove of Fenichka?

NIKOLAI: I hope you don't mind too much, Arkady.

ARKADY: Mind? Why in God's name should I mind?

NIKOLAI: Well, because . . . well, I just thought that . . . Anyhow, anyhow, the real reason I brought her into the house – and I want you to know that I do, I do care very much for the girl, Arkady – I thought it only proper and correct that she ought to be in the house after – (*Pause*) – she'd had the baby.

ARKADY: Baby?

NIKOLAI: Hers and mine.

ARKADY: You mean –?

NIKOLAI: A boy.

ARKADY: You and –?

NIKOLAI: Six months old.

ARKADY: I have a new brother.

NIKOLAI: Half-brother.

ARKADY: Half-brother.

NIKOLAI: Mitya.

ARKADY: Mitya!

NIKOLAI: Mitya. Now you know it all. Actually he's the image of me.

(ARKADY *suddenly laughs, throws his arms around his father*.)

ARKADY: Father, that is the best news ever!

NIKOLAI: Is it?

ARKADY: Of course it is! You're a sly old rascal but I think you're great. Congratulations!

NIKOLAI: You're not angry?

ARKADY: Angry? For God's sake, Father, I'm delighted for you!

NIKOLAI: Thank you, son. Thank you. We'll not talk about it before Pavel. I'm not sure he quite approves of the whole thing. You know Pavel with his silly notions of class and public decorum.

(PAVEL *and* BAZAROV *enter left*.)

We can talk later.

(BAZAROV, *a student, dark, lean, intense. He senses that he is an outsider politically and socially in this house – hence the arrogance and curt manner*.)

ARKADY: There he is! Come on, Bazarov! Come over here. Uncle Pavel you've obviously met – Pavel Petrovich Kirsanov. And this is my father, Nikolai Petrovich Kirsanov. Yevgeny Vassilyich Bazarov.

(BAZAROV *bows formally*.)

NIKOLAI: You are most welcome to this house, Yevgeny Vassilyich. I hope you can stay with us for most of the summer and I hope you don't find us very dull company.

PAVEL: Do you remember a Doctor Bazarov in Father's old division? That's his father, he tells me.

NIKOLAI: Really? My goodness, it's a small . . . it's a . . .

PAVEL: Extraordinaire, n'est ce pas?

NIKOLAI: Indeed. And you're going to be a doctor, too? Great. Splendid. Sit down. Sit down. You must be tired after your journey.

BAZAROV: I'd prefer to stand.

NIKOLAI: Of course. Stand. Naturally. Stretch your legs. By all means – stand . . . Now to organize our lives. Let's have tea

8

out here. Then you young men can have a rest and we'll eat about seven o'clock. All right? Piotr! He deliberately hides on me, you know. It's gone far beyond a joke. Dunyasha! Oh, you've no idea how difficult things are becoming. I'm not exaggerating, Pavel, am I? The old system – of course it had its failings. But now? – now I give all my land to the peasants to farm – *give* it to them. Will they even farm it for themselves? I wish you'd take an interest in it all, Arkady. It's becoming too much for me at my time of – sorry. (*To* DUNYASHA.) Ah, Dunyasha. Bring the samovar out here.

PAVEL: Cocoa for me, *s'il vous plaît*.

NIKOLAI: And a bottle of that black sherry in the sideboard. The young men may wish to – to – to dissipate!

(DUNYASHA *is staring at* BAZAROV.)

ARKADY: Do you wish to dissipate, Bazarov? We would love to dissipate, Father.

NIKOLAI: Dunyasha!

DUNYASHA: Sorry, sir?

NIKOLAI: Black sherry. In the sideboard. And glasses.

(*She goes into the house.*)

What's the matter with that girl? And how is your father, Yevgeny Vassilyich?

(BAZAROV *looks blankly at him. Pause.*)

Your father – is he well?

BAZAROV: I suppose so. I haven't seen him for three years.

NIKOLAI: He has been away – has he? – travelling?

BAZAROV: Not that I know of.

NIKOLAI: Ah.

BAZAROV: I haven't seen him for three years because I haven't been home since I went to the university.

(*Silence.*)

ARKADY: (*Quickly*) Let me tell you about this character. He won the gold medal for oratory again this year – the third year in succession.

NIKOLAI: Wonderful!

ARKADY: And he is also – (*To* BAZAROV) – no, don't try to stop me – he is also president of the philosophical society and

9

editor of the magazine. It's an astonishing radical publication – the college authorities banned both issues this year! We were brought before the disciplinary council – remember? 'Revolutionaries! Damned revolutionaries!'

NIKOLAI: Oratory is an excellent discipline; excellent. I approve very strongly of – of – of – of oratory.

PAVEL: On what do you . . . orate?

BAZAROV: Politics. Philosophy.

PAVEL: They have something in common, have they?

ARKADY: Come on, Uncle Pavel. You know they have.

PAVEL: (*To* BAZAROV) And your philosophy is?

ARKADY: Nihilism.

PAVEL: Sorry?

ARKADY: Nihilism, Uncle Pavel. Bazarov is a Nihilist. So am I.

NIKOLAI: Interesting word that. I imagine it comes from the Latin – *nihil* – nothing. Does it mean somebody who respects nothing? No, it doesn't.

ARKADY: Someone who looks at everything critically.

PAVEL: If there's a difference.

ARKADY: There's a significant difference, Pavel. Don't be so precious.

PAVEL: Me? – precious? Good Lord.

ARKADY: Nihilism begins by questioning all received ideas and principles no matter how venerated those ideas and principles are. And that leads to the inevitable conclusion that the world must be made anew. (*To* BAZAROV.) That's a fairly accurate summary of our stance, isn't it?

(BAZAROV *shrugs indifferently and spreads his hands.*)

PAVEL: So you believe only in science?

ARKADY: We don't *believe* in anything. You can't believe in science any more than you can believe in the weather or farming or swimming.

NIKOLAI: I can tell you farming isn't what it used to be. In the past five years, the advances I've seen in farming techniques—

ARKADY: I wish you would stop trying to divert me with your juvenile asides, Father.

NIKOLAI: I am sorry.

PAVEL: A simple question: if you reject all accepted principles and all accepted precepts, what basis of conduct have you?

ARKADY: I don't understand what the simple question means.

PAVEL: On what basis do you conduct your life?

ARKADY: If something is useful – keep it. If it is not useful – out it goes. And the most useful thing we can do is repudiate, renounce, reject.

PAVEL: Everything?

ARKADY: Everything without use.

PAVEL: All accepted conventions, all art, all science?

ARKADY: What use are they? Out.

PAVEL: Civilization has just been disposed of, Nikolai.

NIKOLAI: But surely, Arkady, surely rejection means destruction; and surely we must construct, too?

ARKADY: Our first priority is to make a complete clearance. At this point in our evolution we have no right to indulge in the gratification of our own personal whims.

NIKOLAI: I don't think I had whims in mind, Arkady.

ARKADY: At times it's difficult to know what you have in mind, Father.

PAVEL: And when do you begin to preach this gospel publicly?

ARKADY: We're activists. We aren't preachers, are we, Bazarov? We are not going to—

PAVEL: Aren't you preaching now? (*To* NIKOLAI.) This is all nonsense; weary old materialistic nonsense I've heard a hundred times.

ARKADY: We know there is starvation and poverty; we know our politicians take bribes; we know the legal system is corrupt. We know all that. And we are tired listening to the 'liberals' and the 'progressives'—

PAVEL: So you have identified all society's evils—

NIKOLAI: Let him finish, Pavel.

PAVEL: I would prefer Yevgeny Vassilyich would do his own talking. (*To* ARKADY.) But you intend to do nothing constructive yourselves?

BAZAROV: We intend to do nothing constructive ourselves.

PAVEL: Just abuse people who do.

BAZAROV: Just abuse people who do.

PAVEL: And that's called Nihilism.

BAZAROV: And that's called Nihilism. Is this riveting discussion nearly over?

PAVEL: *Incroyable*! Let me see have I got it right—

NIKOLAI: I'm sure you've got it right, Pavel. Let's leave it for now.

PAVEL: First our saviours will demolish the country and then they will remake the country. But suppose some simple person were to suggest that our saviours were just bletherskites – gold-medal bletherskites?

BAZAROV: My grandfather was a serf, Pavel Petrovich. I believe I have some knowledge of the Russian people.

PAVEL: I'm sure you have a very—

BAZAROV: Indeed I believe I have at least as accurate and as sympathetic an understanding of their needs and of their mute aspirations as those absurd provincial aristocrats who affect English clothes and English customs; who believe they are civilized just because they speak cliché French; who talk endlessly about Mother Russia but who sit on their backsides and do sweet nothing for the '*bien public*' as they call it.

PAVEL: I suspect you're deliberately trying to—

BAZAROV: Words that come so easily to lips like yours – liberalism, progress, principles, civilization – they have no meaning in Russia. They are imported words. Russia doesn't need them. But what Russia does need – and action will provide it, Pavel Petrovich, action, not words – what Russia does need is bread in the mouth. But before you can put bread in the mouth, you have got to plough the land – deep.

NIKOLAI: He's right, you know: ploughing is a very important part of the farming cycle. (*To* ARKADY.) Sorry. I didn't—

PAVEL: So the two of you are going to reform Russia.

BAZAROV: Remake Russia. Yes.

PAVEL: By force?

BAZAROV: (*Shrugs*) If necessary.

ARKADY: All that's needed is a few people with total dedication. It was a penny candle that burned Moscow down, Uncle Pavel.

NIKOLAI: That's quite true, you know.

PAVEL: For God's sake, Nikolai, you know nothing about it!

NIKOLAI: I beg your pardon, Pavel – it *was* a penny candle burned Moscow down. That is an historical fact. Father was able to quote chapter and verse on it.

(*To* FENICHKA *and* DUNYASHA *who have entered with a tray and samovar.*)

Ah! Fenichka! Good! Great! Splendid! And beautifully timed – just when we had all come to a close understanding of one another's position. Have you the sherry? Excellent. (*To* DUNYASHA.) Just leave the tray there. Thank you. Thank you. You haven't met Arkady's friend, have you, Fenichka? Yevgeny Vassilyich Bazarov.

BAZAROV: Pleased to meet you.

FENICHKA: You're welcome.

BAZAROV: Thank you.

ARKADY: Dr Bazarov – almost.

FENICHKA: Welcome, Doctor.

NIKOLAI: (*To* DUNYASHA *who is staring at* BAZAROV)

Dunyasha, will you put the tray down on the seat, please?

DUNYASHA: Oh yes – yes, yes, yes.

NIKOLAI: I think this is yours, Pavel (*Cocoa.*).

PAVEL: Thanks.

(*As the cups are being passed round* ARKADY *has a private word with* FENICHKA.)

ARKADY: Congratulations.

(*She looks puzzled.*)

On the baby.

FENICHKA: Oh. (*She looks quickly towards* NIKOLAI.)

ARKADY: He's just told me.

FENICHKA: He wasn't sure how you'd react.

ARKADY: I'm pleased for you both.

FENICHKA: Thank you.

(NIKOLAI *is aware of this private conversation.*)

NIKOLAI: You're sitting with us, Fenichka, aren't you?

FENICHKA: Not just now. I've got to bath Mitya and put him to bed. I'll join you later.

NIKOLAI: Please do.

(FENICHKA *leaves.*)

DUNYASHA: Can I get you anything else?

NIKOLAI: That's everything, I think, Dunyasha.

(*She is gazing at* BAZAROV *and does not move.*)

Thank you.

(*She goes.*)

There's something the matter with that girl today. Now to organize our lives. Let me tell you what plans we have in store for you. The first formal engagement is on Monday week. It's a rather long and convoluted story that—

PAVEL: It's quite simple: he's having a welcome-home party for you.

ARKADY: Great.

NIKOLAI: Some weeks ago quite out of the blue I had a visit from a young lady called Anna Sergeyevna Odintsov. (*To* BAZAROV.) An unusual name, isn't it? – Odintsov. Are you familiar with it?

BAZAROV: (*Not listening*) No.

NIKOLAI: It was unknown to me, too, I must confess. Anyhow it transpires that the young lady's mother, may she rest in peace, and my good wife, may she rest in peace, were very close friends when they were young girls. But, as so often happens, they lost touch with one another shortly after they got married. But to cut a long story short. Anna Sergeyevna was rummaging in an attic in her home—

PAVEL: Could I have sugar?

NIKOLAI: —and she came across a bundle of letters written by your good mother, Maria, to her old friend – well, her young friend then. And Anna Sergeyevna had the kind thought that I might like to have these letters since they contain many references to myself. (*To* BAZAROV.) Arkady's mother and I were, as we say, walking out at the time.

BAZAROV: (*Not listening*) Yes?

PAVEL: Cream, please.

NIKOLAI: I'd be delighted to have the letters, I said. So the following week Anna Sergeyevna Odintsov called on us again and handed over Maria's epistles and spent a very agreeable couple of hours with us – didn't she, Pavel?

PAVEL: I found her very . . . measured.

NIKOLAI: Did you think so?

PAVEL: And emotionally dehydrated.

ARKADY: Uncle Pavel!

PAVEL: Oh yes.

NIKOLAI: Well, I liked her very much.

ARKADY: What age is she?

NIKOLAI: I'm very bad at that sort of thing. I would imagine she
    might—

PAVEL: Twenty-nine.

ARKADY: Interesting.

NIKOLAI: Oh yes, an interesting lady.

PAVEL: Enormously wealthy. With a huge estate. And a widow.

ARKADY: *Very* interesting.

NIKOLAI: Very – ? Oh, I see what you mean now. Very good.
    Very good. What else do we know about her? She lives with
    an eccentric old aunt, Princess Something-or-other.

PAVEL: Olga.

NIKOLAI: Olga. And she has a young sister called – what's the
    young sister's name?

PAVEL: Katerina.

NIKOLAI: That's it – Katya. All three are coming on Monday
    week. (*Pause.*) And we'll have a wonderful party. (*Pause.*)
    And we'll all have a wonderful time. (*Pause.*) Won't we?

PAVEL: If you'll excuse me. I get a headache when I sit too long
    in the sun.

NIKOLAI: We have a meeting with the new estate manager in half
    an hour, Pavel.

PAVEL: I'll be in my room.

NIKOLAI: I'll join you in a few minutes.
    (*As he exits* PAVEL *puts his hand on Arkady's shoulder and pats
    it. Then he leaves.*)
    Nothing Pavel likes better than a vigorous discussion, plenty
    of thrust and parry. We're inclined to go to seed here in the
    wilds, Yevgeny.

BAZAROV: Yes.

ARKADY: (*Quickly*) What were the letters like?

NIKOLAI: Letters?

ARKADY: The letters Mother wrote to her friend about you.

NIKOLAI: Oh, they were . . . oh-ho, I'm afraid they were a bit naughty in places . . . very naughty in fact . . . in fact a few of them were very naughty indeed . . . You never really know what people are like, do you? We all have our codes. We all have our masks.

(PIOTR *enters left. He is nineteen, exceedingly cocky and self-assured. He knows* NIKOLAI *is fond of him and he plays on that. He wears a single ear-ring and his hair is done in various vivid colours.*)

PIOTR: You wanted me, sir?

NIKOLAI: Yes, Piotr?

PIOTR: You sent for me, sir.

NIKOLAI: I did?

PIOTR: Dunyasha said you wanted me.

NIKOLAI: I'm sure I did, Piotr; and I'm sure you didn't hear me. (*To* BAZAROV.) Piotr's hearing is erratic.

PIOTR: (*Aggrieved*) My hearing is perfect, sir. I was slaving in the stables. You could scream and I wouldn't hear you there, sir.

NIKOLAI: Never mind now, Piotr. Look who's here.

PIOTR: I know. I saw the carriage. Welcome home, Arkady.

ARKADY: Thank you, Piotr.

NIKOLAI: And this is another young graduate – well, almost a graduate – Yevgeny Vassilyich.

PIOTR: Sir.

BAZAROV: Hello.

NIKOLAI: Do you like his multicoloured hair?

ARKADY: It's what all the young dudes in Petersburg are wearing, Piotr.

PIOTR: I know that. But nobody around this place does.

NIKOLAI: And his single blue ear-ring?

PIOTR: Pardon me, sir – turquoise.

NIKOLAI: Forgive me, Piotr – turquoise. I beg your pardon. (*Waving him away.*) No, I don't want you now. Yes, I do. Take this tray away with you. And get the carriage out and bring it round to the back.

PIOTR: Certainly, sir. No sooner said.

NIKOLAI: 'No sooner said'! He has my heart broken. (PIOTR *exits.*)

And I'm very fond of him – he's so cheeky. (*Looks at watch.*)
Five thirty. I must run. Show Yevgeny where the guest-room is.
Have a wash. Walk around. Take a rest. Do whatever pleases
you. We'll eat at seven. And welcome again – both of you.
(*He leaves.*

*ARKADY is annoyed with his friend: he thinks his exchange
with PAVEL was too personal. BAZAROV is unaware of this. He
goes to the samovar.*)

BAZAROV: How did your father get that limp?

ARKADY: Broken leg when he was young. Badly set.

BAZAROV: I like him. He's a decent man. An astute bird, too.
What's the relationship between him and the blonde woman?

ARKADY: Fenichka. She's his mistress.

BAZAROV: Ah. I got a whiff of something there.

ARKADY: I suppose that's one way of putting it.

BAZAROV: Have they known each other long?

ARKADY: She has a child by him.

BAZAROV: Good-looking woman. A nice self-awareness about
her. Fenichka.

ARKADY: He should marry her.

BAZAROV: Who needs marriage? Your father's a lot more
progressive than you, my friend. I suspect – just glancing
round the yard – I suspect he's not the most organized
landowner in Russia. But his heart's in the right place. Tea?

ARKADY: I thought you were a bit severe on Uncle Pavel.

BAZAROV: God, what a freak that is!

ARKADY: It sounded like a personal attack – cliché French – all
that stuff.

BAZAROV: Have you any idea of the shock it is to walk into a
place like this, miles from anywhere, and to be confronted by
that – that decaying dandy? And all those archaic theories
about 'civilization' and a 'basis of conduct'! He's a bloody
absurdity!

ARKADY: He was considered to be the most handsome officer in
the army in his day; and the best gymnast.

BAZAROV: No, he's not absurd – he's grotesque.

ARKADY: He was made a captain when he was only twenty-one.
Women just threw themselves at him. And he has travelled

everywhere and read everything. And he speaks three or four
languages. And he dined once with Louis Philippe; and he
and the Duke of Wellington corresponded on and off for years

BAZAROV: (*Imitating* PAVEL) Good heavens.

ARKADY: And then, when he was in his mid-twenties, he fell in
love – one of those passions that consumes totally. I
remember hearing the story when I was very young. She was
a princess; married; with a child.

(DUNYASHA *appears on the veranda and shakes out a table-
cloth.* BAZAROV *pretends to think she is waving at him and
waves back at her.* DUNYASHA *withdraws coyly.*)

BAZAROV: That Dunyasha lady has a sporty eye.

ARKADY: And she had this radiant golden hair and when she let
it down 'it fell to below her knees', like Rapunzel in the fairy
story. They lived together for a while. Then she got tired of
him. Cleared off to Germany, France, somewhere. Just
disappeared. He followed her, of course; pursued her
frantically for ten years all over Europe. Then he got word
that she had died, apparently in some kind of demented
state, in some shabby boarding-house in Paris.

BAZAROV: Where else.

ARKADY: Oh yes, there was another detail.

BAZAROV: (*Pretended eagerness*) What was that?

ARKADY: Early in their affair he gave her a ring with a sphinx
engraved on the stone. And the family legend has it that she
said to him, 'Why the sphinx?'

BAZAROV: 'You are that sphinx.'

ARKADY: That's right! That's what he said! And exactly seven
weeks after she died a package was delivered to his club. He
opened it up and inside—

BAZAROV: —was the ring.

ARKADY: Yes. That was in 1848, the year Mother died. Father
was alone here then, lost without his Maria. He asked Uncle
Pavel to join him. And he came. And he has lived here, really
like a recluse, ever since, in a sort of profound and perpetual
melancholy . . . I'm very fond of him. I think he's a good
man, Uncle Pavel.

(*Pause.*)

BAZAROV: You astonish me at times, Arkady. I tell myself that you *are* maturing politically, intellectually, emotionally. And then you come out with the greatest load of romantic hogwash that quite honestly alarms me. Rapunzel – radiant golden hair – passions that consume totally—

ARKADY: If you knew Pavel as well as I—

BAZAROV: Look at him dispassionately. The shape and character of his entire life was determined by a single, ridiculous passion. And when that ridiculous passion wasn't reciprocated – what happens? He sinks into a 'profound and perpetual melancholy'! For the rest of his life! Because of a crazy woman! That's the behaviour of an imbecile! (*Beginning to win* ARKADY *over.*) Let me give you Dr Bazarov's Principles Concerning the Proper Ordering of the Relationships between Men and Women.

ARKADY: I must write these deathless words down.

BAZAROV: One. Romantic love is a fiction.
Two. There is nothing at all mysterious between the sexes. The relationship is quite simply physical.
Three. To believe that the relationship should be dressed up in the trappings of chivalry is crazy. The troubadours were all lunatics.
Four. If you fancy a woman, any woman, always, always try to make love to her. If you want to dissipate, dissipate.

ARKADY: Poor old Father – I was a bit sharp with him.

BAZAROV: And if you can't make love to that particular woman, so what? Believe Dr Bazarov – there are plenty more fish in the sea.

ARKADY: You're a bastard, Bazarov. You know that?

BAZAROV: Admit it. Am I not right?

ARKADY: (*Thawing*) A perverse bastard – that's what you are.

BAZAROV: Draw up a list of all the women you'd like to make love to – no commitment, no responsibilities – just for the sheer pleasure of it.

ARKADY: Keep your voice down, man.

BAZAROV: No complications of 'love', romance, none of that rubbish.

ARKADY: That's a game for undergraduates. I'm a graduate – remember?

BAZAROV: A quick roll in the hay – great fun – goodbye.

ARKADY: All gross pigs, you medicals.

BAZAROV: I'll start you off. Natasha Petrova.

ARKADY: Natasha who?

BAZAROV: The inconstancy of the man! Your first year in Petersburg – the landlady's big red-headed daughter – Natasha the Greyhound!

ARKADY: Come on, Bazarov. There was nothing at all to that.

BAZAROV: You wrote a sonnet to her.

ARKADY: I never did!

BAZAROV: 'Could I outstrip the beauty of that form
That haunts these dark and wretched hours called life—'

ARKADY: All right – all right! That was just a passing—

BAZAROV: Exactly. Quick roll – great fun – goodbye. She's number one. Dunyasha?

ARKADY: Dunyasha? – here?

BAZAROV: On the list or not?

ARKADY: I never really thought about her in that—

BAZAROV: A sporty eye, an open heart, a great armful.

ARKADY: Now that you mention her, I suppose she—

BAZAROV: She's elected; number two. Anna Sergeyevna?

ARKADY: Who's she?

BAZAROV: The woman who's coming for the party on Monday week.

ARKADY: We've never seen her.

BAZAROV: Who cares?

ARKADY: She's wealthy.

BAZAROV: Twenty-nine years of age.

ARKADY: A huge estate.

BAZAROV: And a widow.

ARKADY: Is that important?

BAZAROV: The experience, man.

ARKADY: Good point. What do you say?

BAZAROV: If only for the experience – number three. And her young sister – Katya?

ARKADY: I think so.

BAZAROV: Vote. Yes or no.

ARKADY: Katya? I like Katya. I fancy Katya. Yes.

BAZAROV: Elected. Good. Four so far.

(FENICHKA *appears on the veranda.*)

FENICHKA: Yevgeny Vassilyich!

BAZAROV: Hello.

FENICHKA: The baby has some kind of a rash on the back of his neck. Would you take a look at it for me?

BAZAROV: It would be a pleasure. Where is he?

FENICHKA: He's back here in the kitchen.

BAZAROV: I'm on my way. (*To* ARKADY.) My first professional job.

ARKADY: I'd be sure to get a second opinion, Fenichka.

BAZAROV: (*Softly*) Would you say that Fenichka is a possible number five?

ARKADY: Bazarov, you—!

BAZAROV: In jest, my friend, in jest.

(*He goes towards the veranda where* FENICHKA *is waiting for him.*)

ARKADY: (*Calls*) Even in jest! Bazarov, for God's sake, man.

(BAZAROV *turns at the steps and smiles back at him. Then he and* FENICHKA *go into the house.*)

SCENE 2

Early June. After dinner.

NIKOLAI and KATYA are playing duets on the piano in the living-room. KATYA is eighteen, open, spirited, garrulous. FENICHKA is standing beside the piano turning the pages on NIKOLAI's instructions. BAZAROV is outside on the veranda, leaning across the rail, slowly eating a dish of ice-cream. PAVEL is sitting alone and remote downstage right; reading. ANNA is sitting downstage left, listening to the music. She is an elegant, carefully groomed, circumspect woman. She deliberately lives within certain emotional limits and is wary of any intrusion inside them or any excursion outside them. The PRINCESS is sitting upstage right, beneath an enormous parasol which partly conceals her. Now and then she emerges from behind it. She is very old, very eccentric, very energetic. She constantly and vigorously masticates imaginary food and every so often brushes imaginary crumbs from her sleeve and skirt.

Just before the music comes to an end NIKOLAI calls:

NIKOLAI: Wonderful, Katya. Terrific. Don't stop. Let's do it again from the beginning. Splendid. Two-and-three-and—
  (*They begin the piece again and keep playing throughout the early part of the scene.*
  ARKADY rushes through the living-room and out into the garden, carrying a dish of ice-cream. He is very elated.)

ARKADY: (*As he passes behind BAZAROV*) Get yourself some more ice-cream before it all melts.
  (*He leaps down the steps.*)

BAZAROV: (*As ARKADY crosses before him*) I think the dehydrated widow fancies you.

ARKADY: Doing well, amn't I?

BAZAROV: Give her a message for me.

ARKADY: What?

BAZAROV: Tell her I'd like to do my anatomy practical on her.

ARKADY: Cut that out, Bazarov.

BAZAROV: I'm sure she'd agree.
  (*ARKADY crosses over to the PRINCESS.*)

22

ARKADY: Can I get you anything, Princess Olga?

PRINCESS: (*Emerging*) Cat.

ARKADY: Sorry?

PRINCESS: I smell cat.

ARKADY: Cat?

PRINCESS: Cat-cat-cat. Damn place must be overrun with them. Shoot them all! Shoot them! Shoot them! They'll overrun you if you don't. My father told me that.

(*She vanishes behind the parasol. He goes to* ANNA.)

ANNA: It's best to pay no attention to her.

ARKADY: She sounds so furious.

ANNA: Ignore her. She lives quite contentedly in her own world.

ARKADY: There you are. (*Offers ice-cream.*) I'm afraid it's gone a bit soft.

ANNA: You have it.

ARKADY: I've had enough. Go ahead. There's plenty more. Loads of it. We eat it all the time here. In the summer. God, she's really a magnificent pianist, Katya.

ANNA: She's very competent; no more than that.

ARKADY: And she can sight-read brilliantly. I love that piece. I remember Father and Mother playing it together when I was very small. I'm sure you play, too?

ANNA: No.

ARKADY: Yes, you do. You're being modest.

ANNA: I don't, Arkady.

ARKADY: I'm sure you're a brilliant pianist.

ANNA: No.

ARKADY: I don't believe you. And I'm told you're a painter.
(*She shakes her head.*)
Yes, you are. Katya told me. She says you're terrific with water-colours.

ANNA: Katerina exaggerates.

ARKADY: Bazarov and I are going to visit his parents soon, maybe at the end of next week. I was wondering if we could call on you on our way there?

ANNA: We'd be glad to see you.

ARKADY: Great! Tomorrow, maybe? Are you sure that's all right?

ANNA: He looks like a painter. Is he artistic?

23

ARKADY: Uncle Pavel?

ANNA: Your friend – who believes in nothing.

ARKADY: Bazarov? He's a total philistine! (*Calls.*) We're talking about you!

(BAZAROV *points to his ears, points into the living-room: he cannot hear above the music.*)

(*Shouts*) Anna Sergeyevna wants to know – (*He gives up.*) It doesn't matter.

ANNA: (*Beckons*) Come and join us.

ARKADY: Keep him off politics or he'll give you a boring lecture. I'm a Nihilist, too, you know; like Bazarov.

ANNA: (*Watching* BAZAROV *approach*) Really?

ARKADY: We've a very active cell in Petersburg. There aren't all that many of us but we're absolutely, totally dedicated. Anna wants to know if you're artistic!

ANNA: Arkady says you're a philistine.

ARKADY: He's the worst kind of philistine – he's a scientist.

BAZAROV: What is art for?

ARKADY: (*To* ANNA) I told you.

BAZAROV: Is it necessary?

(ANNA'*s attention has switched to* BAZAROV. *In an attempt to hold her* ARKADY *launches into his monologue. While he lectures,* ANNA *and* BAZAROV *conduct a mute dialogue*; '*Sit here*' – '*No, thanks*' – '*There's a stool*' – '*I'd prefer to stand*' – '*There's a chair*' – '*I'm fine*' – *etc.*)

ARKADY: And the answer to that is: what does the word necessary mean in that context? Is that dish necessary? – that tree? – that cloud formation? We're not exactly in unison on this issue, Bazarov and I. He believes that Nihilism and art are seldom compatible. I don't. But I believe that at this point in our history and in our sociological development it would be wrong for us now to channel our depleted energies into artistic endeavour, not because there is anything intrinsically wrong, or indeed right, with artistic endeavour – but I believe that whatever energies we can muster now have got to be poured into the primary and enormous task of remaking an entire society and that imperative is not only a social obligation but perhaps even a moral obligation and

indeed it is not improbable that the execution of that task
may even have elements of . . . of artistic pursuit . . . or so
it seems to me . . .
(*He tails off in some confusion, unsure that he has made his
point, any point, unsure that he has impressed* ANNA, *unsure that
she has even listened to him.*
Pause.)

PRINCESS: (*Suddenly emerging*) My father always said that the
quickest and most efficient way to break in a difficult young
horse was to hit him over the head with a crow-bar. (*She
demonstrates.*) Bang between the ears! Ha-ha. He was right,
you know. I've done it myself. And it works! It works! It
works!
(*She vanishes again.*
Pause.)

BAZAROV: Lively music, isn't it?

ANNA: So you're not a total philistine.
(BAZAROV *shrugs.*)

BAZAROV: Silly word.

ARKADY: What word?

BAZAROV: Philistine.

ARKADY: No, it's not. It's a precise word.

ANNA: Art can at least help us to know and understand people,
can't it?

BAZAROV: Living does that. (*Laying down ice-cream dish.*) That
was good.

ANNA: Not to the same extent; not in any depth.
(DUNYASHA *enters and picks up various dishes around the lawn.*)

BAZAROV: What is there to understand in depth? All men are
similar physically and intellectually. Each has a brain, a
spleen, heart, lungs. Intellectually? – darker and lighter
shadings, that's all. We're like trees in the forest. Ask any
botanist. Know one birch, know them all.
(DUNYASHA *is about to pick up the dish beside* ANNA.)

ANNA: I'm not finished yet.

DUNYASHA: Sorry, Miss.

BAZAROV: And Dunyasha is the most wholesome and
uncomplicated birch-tree in the whole of Russia.

DUNYASHA: What does that mean?

BAZAROV: It means that you're beautiful and desirable.

ARKADY: Don't listen to him, Dunyasha. Uncle Pavel says he's a bletherskite.

(DUNYASHA *loves this. She gives a great whoop of laughter.*)

DUNYASHA: He did not, did he? A bletherskite! That's great! That's what he is all right!

(*She goes off laughing.*)

BAZAROV: (*Calls*) I still think you're beautiful.

ANNA: So there is no difference between a stupid person and an intelligent person, between a good person and a bad person?

BAZAROV: Of course there is, just as there is a difference between a sick person and a healthy person. The man with tuberculosis has the same *kind* of lungs as you and I but they are in a different condition; and as medicine advances we know how to correct that condition. Moral disease, moral imbalance has different causes – our educational system, religious superstition, heredity, the polluted moral atmosphere our society breathes. But remake society and you eradicate *all* disease.

ANNA: Physical and moral?

BAZAROV: All.

ANNA: (*To* ARKADY) Does he believe that? (*To* BAZAROV.) That if you reform society—

BAZAROV: Remake.

ANNA: Then all illness, all evil, all stupidity disappear?

BAZAROV: Because in our remade society the words stupid and clever, good and bad, will have lost the meaning you invest them with, will probably come to have no meaning at all. Do they not play polkas in the houses of the gentry?

ANNA: (*To* ARKADY) What do you think?

ARKADY: I agree with Bazarov. Bazarov's right.

(ANNA *looks keenly at* BAZAROV.)

ANNA: (*Suddenly to* ARKADY) Could I have some more of that ice-cream?

ARKADY: (*He jumps to his feet, eager to serve*) Wonderful, isn't it? I made it myself. Ice-cream, Uncle Pavel?

PAVEL: What's that?

ARKADY: Ice-cream – do you want some?

BAZAROV: 'Good heavens, no'.

PAVEL: Good heavens, no.

ARKADY: (*Coldly to* BAZAROV) What about you?

BAZAROV: Not for me.

(ARKADY *goes to the* PRINCESS.)

ARKADY: Princess, would you like—

(*She emerges momentarily and scowls at him.*)

PRINCESS: Would I like what? What would I like?

ARKADY: Sorry.

(*He flees. Trips on the veranda steps.*)

ANNA: He's such a nice young man.

BAZAROV: You have unbalanced him.

ARKADY: (*Calls above the piano music*) Anybody for ice-cream?

KATYA: Me, Arkady. Please.

ARKADY: Fenichka?

(*She signals no. He goes to her and dances her round the room in time to the music.* ANNA *claps.*)

ANNA: (*Calls*) Very good, Arkady! Lovely!

BAZAROV: Exquisite.

ANNA: He's a very good dancer.

BAZAROV: (*Sharply*) Altogether he's such a nice young man.

ANNA: (*Calls*) Beautiful, Arkady. Very elegant.

ARKADY: Can't hear you.

BAZAROV: He can't take his eyes off you.

ANNA: Do you dance?

BAZAROV: No.

ANNA: I love dancing.

BAZAROV: Naturally. All aristocrats love dancing.

ANNA: I've told you, Yevgeny – I'm not an aristocrat. Tell me more about your Nihilism.

BAZAROV: It's not mine. I don't possess it like an estate. Tell me what you believe in.

ANNA: Routine; order; discipline.

BAZAROV: That's how you conduct your life, not what you believe in.

ANNA: It's adequate for me.

BAZAROV: Because you have no beliefs or because your beliefs have no passion?

ANNA: Passion is a luxury. I make no excursions outside what I know and can handle.

BAZAROV: These new psychiatrists would say that you avoid belief because belief demands commitment and you're afraid of commitment. And you're afraid of commitment because it would demand everything of you. And because you're not prepared to give everything, you give nothing. And you excuse yourself by calling passion a luxury but you know in your heart that your excuse is a lie.

ANNA: I'm not a liar, Yevgeny Vassilyich.

BAZAROV: I haven't met all that many aristocrats like you in my life—

ANNA: I am not an—

BAZAROV: —but I've noticed that their brain is divided into two equal parts. One part is totally atrophied – the part that might be capable of generosity, enthusiasm, of a thirst for social change, of the desire for risk, for the big gamble, for that dangerous extreme. So they function, these aristocratic cripples, they function with the portion that is left to them; and like some mutilated organ it becomes unnaturally developed and unnaturally active. Hence your aristocrat's irrational obsession with wheat-yield and good-management and productivity and efficiency—

ANNA: And routine and order and discipline. Why are you being so difficult?

BAZAROV: Perhaps I haven't the grace for aristocratic ladies like you.

ANNA: My father, my handsome, gambling, risking, reckless father died when I was twenty. Katerina was only twelve. For two years we lived in penury, the kind of grinding poverty I suspect you have never known, Yevgeny. Then I met a man who was twenty-five years older than me. He was very wealthy, eccentric, a hypochondriac, enormously fat. He had no illusions about himself. He asked me to marry him. I thought about it very carefully and then I said yes. We had six years together. I still miss him. He was a kind man.

BAZAROV: So?

ANNA: So that's all. I suppose I'm trying to – Oh I don't know
why I told you that.

BAZAROV: I'm afraid I'm lost here. I mean – am I to applaud
your circumspection in netting a rich old eccentric – or
commiserate with you on your bereavement? – or
congratulate you on your sudden wealth?

ANNA: Let's not talk about it any more.

BAZAROV: Or are you just teasing my appetite for the full
biography? Because if you are, I'm afraid I find it less than
gripping. But it does have the makings of the kind of rags-to-
riches novelette that someone like Dunyasha, or indeed the
very nice young Arkady, would probably find irresistible.
(ANNA *jumps to her feet and would leave but* BAZAROV *catches
her by the arms.*)
Oh my God, Anna – forgive me – I'm sorry – I'm sorry –
please, please forgive me—
(*The music has stopped. Everybody is aware of the scene, of the
raised voices. Everybody is staring at them.* BAZAROV *realizes
he is holding her and lets her go.*)
(*Lowering his voice*) I've no idea why I said that – it was
unpardonable, unpardonable – I'm sorry – I'm deeply sorry
– please forgive me – please.
(*Silence.* PAVEL, *the only person unaware of the scene, closes his
book and walks slowly across the stage towards* ANNA.)

PAVEL: (*Applauding the pianists*) Bravo! Well done! Lovely!
Thank you. Your sister is a very talented pianist.

ANNA: What are you reading, Pavel Petrovich?

PAVEL: This? Ne vaut pas la peine d'être lu. *The Romance of the
Forest* by an English novelist called Mrs Anna Ward
Radcliffe. A simple lady. But it kills time. Harmlessly.
(*As he goes into the living-room,* ARKADY *enters carrying two
dishes of ice-cream – one for* KATYA *and one for* ANNA.)
(*With distaste*) Good Lord.

ARKADY: Good Lord, it's lovely, Uncle Pavel.
Here we are! Who ordered what? Katya – there you are – one
vanilla ice-cream coated with chocolate dressing and topped
with a single glistening cherry.

KATYA: Thank you, Arkady. Oh, lovely!

BAZAROV: (*Softly to* ANNA) Please forgive me. I'm deeply sorry. (*He exits quickly left.*)

ARKADY: (*To* KATYA) My great pleasure. (*Coming outside.*) And one without dressing for Anna Sergeyevna Odintsov. (KATYA *comes down beside him.*)

KATYA: Did you really make it yourself?

ARKADY: Why the surprise? I'm expert at all foods, amn't I, Bazarov? Where's Bazarov? In the flat we shared I did all the cooking and he did all the washing and cleaning.

KATYA: (*To* ANNA) You're pale. Are you all right?

ANNA: I'm fine – fine – we'll soon have to go, Katerina.

KATYA: No, we're not leaving for some time. I like it here. (NIKOLAI *and* FENICHKA *come down.*)

NIKOLAI: I really enjoyed that. I haven't played piano duets since Maria and I used to sit in there and – (*Recovering*) – oh, not for years and years. Did we go on too long?

ANNA: Not long enough. We had a lovely evening.

NIKOLAI: I hope it's the first of many. It's beginning to get cold. Do you think the Princess is warm enough?

ANNA: She's all right. Anyway it's time we got the carriage ready.

NIKOLAI: Piotr! Piotr! He must be somewhere around. Ah, Prokofyich, would you see to Madam Odintsov's carriage?

PROKOFYICH: Certainly, madam. (ANNA *pushes the parasol aside.*)

ANNA: Time to move, Auntie Olga. We have a long journey before us.

PRINCESS: Long journeys – short journeys – my father always said they all end up in the same place: nowhere, nowhere, nowhere. (ANNA *takes her arm and together they go into the living-room.* ARKADY *watches* ANNA *as she goes.*)

KATYA: You were to show me the litter of pups, Arkady.

ARKADY: Sorry?

KATYA: The litter of pups – you were to show me them.

ARKADY: So I was. We'll go just now. They're in the stable.

KATYA: How many are there?

ARKADY: Four. Would you like one?

KATYA: What do you mean – would I like one? We talked about this all morning and you said I could have the pick of the litter. Don't you remember?

ARKADY: Of course I remember. And it's the pick of the litter you'll get, Katerina.

KATYA: Katya! Katya! Katya! We talked about that, too! I told you I loathe Katerina. Anna's the only one who calls me Katerina.

ARKADY: Sorry, Katya. The pick of the litter – your choice – whatever one you want. Or take two of them. Or three of them. Or take them all.

KATYA: 'Take them all'! You're an awful clown, you know.

ARKADY: Why?

KATYA: Just the way you go on. If you want my honest opinion, I think you're not a very mature person yet.

ARKADY: Really?!

KATYA: But that will come in time.

ARKADY: Oh, good. Then I'll be like you.

KATYA: No, no – always a little behind. But close enough. Come on – Anna wants to leave soon.

(*She leads him off left.* NIKOLAI *and* FENICHKA *move downstage.* DUNYASHA *comes into the living-room and tidies around. She is singing.*)

NIKOLAI: I wouldn't be at all surprised if Arkady has fallen for young Katya. I noticed, when we were playing the piano, she kept watching him.

FENICHKA: I think it's Anna Sergeyevna he likes.

NIKOLAI: Do you think so? Oh, I would hope not. Anna Sergeyevna is a splendid young woman but much too sophisticated for Arkady. Sit down beside me. You must be tired. You had a busy day.

FENICHKA: I was tired earlier but I'm fine now. When are the boys leaving?

NIKOLAI: The end of next week, I believe. And I'm glad – no, not that they're leaving – (*Whispers*) – but that Bazarov is finally going to his parents. Hasn't seen them for three whole years! Can you imagine – not since he started college!

31

FENICHKA: Some people live like that. It doesn't mean he doesn't care for them.

NIKOLAI: That's true. Maybe it's just a matter of being alert to certain sensibilities. He's fond of you – Bazarov.

FENICHKA: Is he?

NIKOLAI: Oh, yes. He's more relaxed with you than with anybody else in the house.

FENICHKA: I like him, too. Strange man.

NIKOLAI: And Arkady's also fond of you, thank heaven!

FENICHKA: I'm very fond of Arkady.

(DUNYASHA *exits. They are alone*.)

NIKOLAI: And of Mitya. Calls him 'little half-brother'.

FENICHKA: I've heard him. It's funny to see them playing together.

NIKOLAI: We had a long talk the other day. We were alone in the garden here. It was like old times – just the two of us. And then do you know what he did out of the blue? He scolded me!

FENICHKA: Arkady?

NIKOLAI: Quite severely. He said I shouldn't have allowed you to live above that laundry for so long.

FENICHKA: (*Becoming embarrassed*) What Arkady doesn't know is that the room above the laundry is the warmest room in the house.

NIKOLAI: It is also damp. Anyhow his point was that you were pregnant and you should have been in the main building; that it was most insensitive of me. And he's right.

FENICHKA: That's all over, Nikolai. I'm in the main house now. You're right – it is getting cold.

NIKOLAI: He said, too, that we should be married. Yes. He had no doubts whatever. He thinks it's ridiculous we're not married. Remarkable, isn't it?

FENICHKA: What is?

NIKOLAI: That that is his attitude. And I found it very reassuring. More than reassuring – encouraging, most encouraging. Wouldn't you agree?

FENICHKA: Oh, yes; most encouraging.

NIKOLAI: And of course Pavel would be in favour. No question about his attitude.

FENICHKA: Has he said that to you?

NIKOLAI: He doesn't have to say it – I know Pavel. Convention – decorum. Oh, yes, Pavel will want the proprieties observed. So, since I now know what Arkady thinks – and unlike his dithering old father he hadn't a moment's hesitation – and since I've always known that Pavel would be in favour—
(FENICHKA *buries her face in her handkerchief and cries.* NIKOLAI *watches her in alarm and bewilderment.*)
Fenichka? Fenichka, what's the matter with –? My God, what have I done wrong? Did I do anything? – did I say anything? Did somebody hurt you? Who hurt you? Please don't cry, Fenichka. Please. Tell me what's the matter with you. Fenichka? Fenichka?
(*She continues to cry. He continues to watch her in bewilderment.*)

SCENE 3

End of June.

ARKADY *and* BAZAROV *are sitting at the dining-room table in Bazarov's home. With them are Bazarov's father,* VASSILY IVANYICH BAZAROV, *and his mother,* ARINA VLASSYEVNA. VASSILY IVANYICH *is in his early sixties, a tall, thin, pipe-smoking man dressed in an old military jacket. He is very ill at ease in the presence of his guests and talks too much – and is aware that he is talking too much – to hide his unease.*

ARINA VLASSYEVNA *is a small, plump woman in her fifties. The first impression is of a quiet, simple country woman. But she is alert to every nuance in the conversation and watches her son and his friend to gauge their reaction to her husband's compulsive talking. Two servants attend the table –* TIMOFEICH, *an old retainer, almost decrepit, and* FEDKA, *a very young boy who is employed only because of the visitors.* FEDKA *is barefooted.*

Lunch has just finished.

VASSILY: Very good question, Arkady Nikolayevich: how do I pass the time? Excellent question. And I will tell you the answer to that question. Timofeich, more blackcurrant tea for our guest.

ARKADY: Just a little. (*To* ARINA.) That was a very nice lunch. Thank you.

ARINA: You're welcome.

    (BAZAROV *gets to his feet and paces around the room.*)

VASSILY: Yevgeny?

BAZAROV: None for me.

ARINA: (*Privately to* BAZAROV) Take another biscuit.

BAZAROV: (*Playfully shaking his head*) Shhh!

ARINA: I'm going to have to fatten you up over the next two months.

    (BAZAROV *responds by puffing out his cheeks and his chest and miming a fat man.*)

VASSILY: How do I pass the time? I'm a bit like ancient Gaul: I'm divided into *tres partes*, as our friend Caesar might put it.

One part is the reader. Another part is the gardener. And the third part is the practising doctor – even though I'm supposed to have retired years ago. Not a day passes but there's a patient at my door. (*To* ARINA.) That wouldn't be incorrect, my pet, would it? And interestingly enough all of those three parts add up to one complete integer. My reading is all medical reading. My gardening is all medical gardening – I believe I have the best garden of medicinal herbs in the whole province. That wouldn't be inaccurate, my pet, would it? Nature itself as healer – it's the answer, you know. As our friend Paracelsus puts it: I trust *in herbis, in verbis et in lapidibus*.

BAZAROV: (*To* ARKADY) Father was a great classical scholar in his day.

VASSILY: Great? I wouldn't say I—

BAZAROV: Won a medal for Latin composition. Silver. When he was only twelve.

VASSILY: I suspect he's mocking me. Are you mocking me?

BAZAROV: Me?

ARINA: Finish your story, Vassily.

VASSILY: Where was I?

BAZAROV: *In herbis, in verbis et in lapidibus.*

VASSILY: Tending my garden, attending my patients, and in my spare time looking after my modest farm. (*To* ARKADY.) I shouldn't say 'my modest farm' – I'm a plebeian, a *homo novus* – Yevgeny's mother is the patrician.

ARINA: Vassily!

(BAZAROV *bows to his mother and kisses her hand.*)

BAZAROV: Her serene highness, Arina Vlassyevna Bazarov.

ARINA: Behave yourself.

VASSILY: For God's sake, Fedka, will you put something on your feet. Timofeich, take this little urchin away and dress him correctly. Arkady Nikolayevich will think he's staying with some sort of primitives.

BAZAROV: Isn't that what we are?

VASSILY: You're very facetious today, young man. But where was I? Yes, talking of medicine. You'll enjoy this. I hear that a retired major about six miles from here is doing a bit of doctoring. So one day, when we meet at the market, this major and I, I said, 'I hear you're in practice, Major?' 'Yes,' he said. 'Where did you qualify?' 'I never qualified,' he said. 'Never? But where did you study your medicine?' 'I never studied medicine.' 'But you practise medicine, Major?' 'Oh, yes. But not for money – just for the good of the community.'

(VASSILY *alone laughs at this.* ARKADY *smiles politely.*)

I love that – 'just for the good of the community' – I really love that. Wonderful man to have around in a typhus epidemic. Incidentally there's a lot of it around . . . typhus . . .

(*Pause.*)

ARINA: (*To* ARKADY) How long did you stay with this – this Madam Odintsov?

ARKADY: A week – (*To* BAZAROV) – wasn't it? I've lost track of time.

BAZAROV: Eight nights.

ARINA: (*To* ARKADY) And you had a nice time there?

ARKADY: It was sheer luxury. We were a bit overwhelmed at first, weren't we?

BAZAROV: Were we?

ARKADY: Well, I was.

BAZAROV: Yes, you were.

ARKADY: A butler in black tails, footmen in livery, scores of maids and servants all over the place. It's really a miniature empire she has there.

ARINA: And she lives with an old aunt and a young sister, this Madam Odintsov?

ARKADY: The old aunt's as mad as a hatter.

ARINA: And the young sister?

ARKADY: Katya is – (*To* BAZAROV) – how would you describe Katya?

BAZAROV: You should have no difficulty. You voted her on your list.

ARINA: List? What list?

ARKADY: (*Embarrassed*) Oh, we made a list, Yevgeny and I – a sort of silly list of – of – of all the pretty girls we know.

36

ARINA: Ah. And Katya is on that list?

ARKADY: She *was* on the list – at the beginning. She was on the first list.

ARINA: I see. She was pretty but she's not pretty now.

ARKADY: Oh, she's pretty, very pretty, isn't she?

BAZAROV: You're not alert to Mother's subtleties, Arkady. When she inquires about 'this – this Madam Odintsov', can't you hear the disapproval in her voice? She has already made up her mind that This Madam Odintsov is what novelists call an adventuress.

ARINA: That's not true.

BAZAROV: (*He hugs her affectionately and laughs*) You're suspicious of her.

ARINA: Don't be silly, Yevgeny.

BAZAROV: You dislike her intensely.

ARINA: I never even heard of the woman until yesterday. He's trying to annoy me.

BAZAROV: In fact you hate The Woman. I know exactly what it means when that little nose twitches like that. It always gives you away.

ARINA: And you? What do you think of her?

(BAZAROV *hugs her again and laughs.*)

BAZAROV: Oh no, no, no, no, no, no, no; you're not going to turn the tables like that, Arina Vlassyevna. Isn't she a cunning little squirrel?

VASSILY: (*To* ARKADY) They're well met, the pair of them.

BAZAROV: The question you really want to ask, Mother – it has tormented you since we arrived yesterday – what you want to ask straight out is: Am I in love with This Madam Odintsov? And the answer is: I don't believe in love, in falling in love, in being in love. Arkady and I spent a pleasant week with Katya and Anna. They're good company. I'm fond of them both. And that's it – *finis fabulae* – (*To* VASSILY) – correct?

VASSILY: Very good, Yevgeny.

BAZAROV: If there is such a thing as a *maladie d'amour* – as the Tailor's Dummy would put it – I'm immune to it. Why don't you direct your loaded questions to Arkady. You're not immune, are you?

37

ARINA: You're too smart for your own good.

(*To* TIMOFEICH *who has entered.*)

Clear the table, will you.

TIMOFEICH: Excuse me, sir. A patient here to see you – a woman.

VASSILY: Can't you see we're still eating, Timofeich? Tell her to come back tomorrow.

(*To* FEDKA *who has entered wearing boots that are much too big for him.*)

That's more like it. Good boy, Fedka.

BAZAROV: What's wrong with the woman?

TIMOFEICH: She's holding herself as if she was in pain. I think she has the gripes.

VASSILY: Dysentery – that's what she has. They call it the gripes about here. *Torminum*, Pliny calls it. Cicero uses the plural – *tormina*. (*To* TIMOFEICH.) Tell her to come back tomorrow morning.

BAZAROV: Let me have a look at her, Father.

VASSILY: No, no; you're on your holidays and—

BAZAROV: Please. I'd like to.

VASSILY: If you'd like to. Very well. Certainly. We'll only be a few—

BAZAROV: I'd prefer to see her by myself.

VASSILY: Off you go. Give her a good shot of opium – you'll find it in my bag on the desk in the study. She'll be most grateful – probably want to pray over you. (BAZAROV *has gone.* VASSILY *calls after him.*) And she'll offer you four eggs as payment. (*To* ARKADY.) Do you know how many eggs I was given last week? One hundred and seventy nine! That's no exaggeration, my pet, is it?

(TIMOFEICH *is clearing the table.* FEDKA *helps him.*)

ARINA: (*Sitting again*) Leave the table for the moment, Timofeich. Fedka, put those raspberries out in the pantry.

(*Both servants leave.*)

ARINA: Are you an only child, too, Arkady?

ARKADY: Yes. No – no – I have a half-brother, Mitya.

ARINA: Is he at college?

ARKADY: He's eight months old.

VASSILY: He has a few weeks to wait yet. (*Raising his glass.*)

Welcome again, Arkady. It's a great pleasure for us to have you here.

ARKADY: Thank you.

VASSILY: A very great pleasure. Isn't that correct, my pet?

ARINA: You're most welcome.

(*Now that they have* ARKADY *alone both parents want desperately to ply him with questions about their son. They move physically closer to him.*)

VASSILY: And I hope you can stay with us until you go back to college.

ARINA: You've forgotten, Vassily – Arkady has graduated.

VASSILY: Forgive me. Of course.

ARINA: And I'm sure he has hundreds of plans for the rest of the summer.

ARKADY: I haven't a plan in the world. I'm – at large!

VASSILY: Then you'll stay. Excellent. It's a delight for us to have Yevgeny's student friends. He usually brings somebody home with him every holiday. Fine young men all of them. And we love the company.

ARINA: Have you known Yevgeny long?

ARKADY: For about a year. We met at the philosophical meetings.

VASSILY: A philosopher, too, is he? Aha! That's a little detail we didn't know, did we?

ARINA: Has he got a girl in Petersburg?

ARKADY: Not that I know of.

VASSILY: I'm sure you have, Arkady; dozens of them.

ARINA: But nobody special?

ARKADY: Yevgeny? No; nobody special.

ARINA: He ate hardly any lunch. Is his appetite always as bad?

ARKADY: He's not very interested in food – maybe because I do the cooking!

ARINA: In this flat you share?

ARKADY: Yes.

ARINA: How many rooms do you have?

ARKADY: Three: bedroom, kitchen, washroom.

ARINA: And how long have you been together?

ARKADY: Oh, for the past year.

ARINA: What does he do about his laundry?

ARKADY: He does it himself. Mine, too. That's the arrangement.

VASSILY: Does he take any exercise?

ARKADY: He walks to lectures. And back. That's about it.

VASSILY: No good. He was always lazy about exercise. Not enough. Not nearly enough.

ARINA: How do you know when you don't know how far it is from the flat to the university? You just don't know. (*To* ARKADY.) And that hotel he mentioned – how many hours a week does he work there?

ARKADY: It varies. Sometimes twenty. Maybe up to thirty.

ARINA: And does he really make enough to feed and clothe himself?

ARKADY: Just about.

ARINA: And pay his fees?

ARKADY: We all live fairly frugally.

ARINA: You know he has never accepted any money from us, never since the first day he—

VASSILY: Arkady Nikolayevich is not interested in our domestic affairs, my pet. Tell me about this revolutionary stuff he was spouting last night, this – this – this—

ARKADY: Nihilism.

VASSILY: That's it. He's not really serious about that, is he? All that rubbish about—

ARKADY: We both are. Deadly serious.

VASSILY: Well, of course it is always valuable – and important, very important – most important to keep reassessing how we order our society. That's a very serious matter.

ARINA: I hope he wasn't serious when we were talking about that Madam Odintsov. He said I disliked her – that I hated her for some reason or other! That was very naughty of him.

ARKADY: He was only joking.

ARINA: I hope so.

ARKADY: You know he—

ARINA: (*Rapidly*) Is he in love with her?

ARKADY: (*Deeply confused*) With Anna? . . . Yevgeny? . . . I – I – how would I know? How do you tell? Maybe. I wouldn't know. I really wouldn't know.

VASSILY: And if he is, that's his own business, Arina. There's just one question I'd like to ask you, Arkady—

ARINA: You've asked Arkady far too many questions. Let him finish his tea.

VASSILY: With respect, my pet, it's you who have asked the questions. My one question is this. In Petersburg – in the university – in the circles you move about in – how would he be assessed academically? What I mean is, would he be considered run-of-the-mill, average, perhaps below average – ?

ARKADY: Yevgeny?! Below average?!

VASSILY: Yes?

ARKADY: Yevgeny is – well, he's the most brilliant student in the university at present, probably one of the most brilliant students ever there.

VASSILY: Yevgeny?

ARKADY: But you must know this yourselves. Yevgeny Vassilyich is unique.

VASSILY: Unique?

ARKADY: Yes. Yes – yes – yes; absolutely unique. And whatever he chooses to do, he's going to have a dazzling future.

VASSILY: Are you listening, Arina?

ARKADY: Oh yes. You have an extra-ordinary son.

(ARINA *cries quietly.* VASSILY *cries quietly at first but then his emotion gets the better of him. Unable to contain himself, he grabs* ARKADY's *hand and kisses it repeatedly.*)

VASSILY: Thank You. (*Kiss.*) Thank you – thank you – thank you. (*Kiss.*) You have made me the happiest man in Russia. (*Kiss.*) And now I'm going to make a confession: I idolize my son. So does his mother. We both do. Worship him. That's not incorrect, my pet, is it? And yet we daren't offer him even the most simple gesture of love, even of affection, because we know he detests any demonstration of emotion whatever. When you arrived here yesterday, I wanted to hold him, to hug him, to kiss him all over. But I daren't. I daren't. And I respect that attitude. It's my own attitude. What we must never forget is that we are talking here about an extra-ordinary man. And an extra-ordinary man cannot be

41

judged by ordinary standards. An extra-ordinary man creates his own standards. Do you understand what I'm trying to say to you, Arkady?

ARKADY: Yes, I do.

VASSILY: A dazzling future – did you hear that, Arina?

ARINA: (*Now recovered*) It's a beautiful day now.

VASSILY: There's no doubt in your mind?

ARKADY: None at all.

ARINA: We should all be out in the garden.

ARKADY: What area he'll move into I can't guess – science, philosophy, medicine, politics – he could be outstanding in any of them. But I do know he's going to be famous.

VASSILY: 'Going to be famous'. Non superbus sed humilis sum. Because some day, Arkady, some day when his biography is written, the following lines will appear: 'He was the son of a simple army doctor who from the beginning recognized his extra-ordinary talents and who despite every discouragement devoted his entire life and every penny he earned to his boy's education.'

(BAZAROV *enters. He is instantly aware of the changed atmosphere and notices* VASSILY *putting away his handkerchief.* ARINA *gets quickly to her feet.*)

ARKADY: Ah, Dr Bazarov on call!

ARINA: It didn't take you long.

ARKADY: Where are the eggs? Did you not deserve a fee?

BAZAROV: The woman had a sprained wrist. All I had to do was strap it.

ARINA: Timofeich!

BAZAROV: What's been happening here?

ARINA: You boys are about to go out and get a bit of colour in your faces. (*To* BAZAROV.) Take Arkady round by the acacia plantation and down to the old mill.

VASSILY: I want to show them my herb garden first.

ARINA: I need you to help me put up new curtains in the study, Vassily.

BAZAROV: There's something going on here.

VASSILY: (*Unable to contain his excitement any longer*) There certainly is something going on here. *Primo*: Arkady

42

Nikolayevich has just decided to spend the rest of the
summer here with us. *Secundo*: I have just decided to invite
Anna and Katya Odintsov to come and have dinner here with
us next Sunday.

ARINA: None of this has been—

VASSILY: Please. Allow me. And *tertio*: I have had a bottle of
champagne in my study for the past three years – and now is
the time to open it.

ARINA: We'll celebrate later, Vassily. We'll have your
champagne at dinner tonight. Can you come into the study
now?

VASSILY: Your curtains are much less important—

ARINA: Now. (*To* BAZAROV *and* ARKADY.) We'll eat at seven.
Have a nice walk.

(*She catches* VASSILY *by the elbow and leads him quickly and
firmly out.*)

BAZAROV: What's this all about?

ARKADY: What's what all about?

BAZAROV: You know damn well what I mean.

ARKADY: Just a moment, Bazarov. Just calm down. Your mother
asked me what plans I had. I said none. Your father then said
– excellent, spend the summer here.

BAZAROV: Fine – fine – fine. Spend the summer here. But you'll
spend it here alone. And what's this about inviting Anna
over here next Sunday?

ARKADY: You're shouting, Bazarov.

BAZAROV: How did that come up? Whose brilliant idea was that?

ARKADY: Your father's.

BAZAROV: Who else! The moment you used the words miniature
empire I could see the peasant eyes dilate. Well, that is not
going to happen!

(VASSILY *puts his head around the door.*)

VASSILY: A patient outside. Sorry – am I intruding? Suffering
from icterus. I have him on a diet of centaurion minus,
carrots and St John's wort. Now I know you don't believe in
medicine, Yevgeny, but I'd welcome your opinion on this.
Not now, of course. Later. Later. Sorry.

(*He withdraws.*)

43

BAZAROV: A whole summer of that? Icterus – do you hear him! – icterus! He couldn't say bloody jaundice, simple bloody jaundice like anybody else. And he's prescribing bloody cabbage water and bloody carrots! For jaundice! The man's a fool! That's what he is – a fool, a fool, a fool! And he's killing that poor bugger out there!

ARKADY: I like him.

BAZAROV: You like him.

ARKADY: He's a nice man.

BAZAROV: My mother's nice. My father's nice. The lunch was nice. Your Uncle Pavel is nice. I've no idea what the word means. Let's look at my father's life and see can we not find a more exact word. What does he do all day? Fusses about his garden. Dabbles in medicine. Bores my mother to death with his endless and pointless prattle. And he'll go on fussing and dabbling and boring until the whole insignificant little episode that was his trivial life is over. We can hardly call that nice, can we? What about futile? – fatuous? – would you risk ridiculous?

ARKADY: And your life is so meaningful, Bazarov, so significant?

BAZAROV: When we were out walking this morning we passed the new cottage that Father has just built for his bailiff and you said, 'Only when every peasant has a decent place like that to live in, only then will Russia be close to perfection. And it's our responsibility to bring that about.' And your face positively glowed with . . . niceness. And I thought to myself, I thought: there really is an unbridgeable chasm between Arkady and me. He thinks he loves those damned peasants. I know I hate them. But I know, too, that when the time comes I will risk everything, everything for them, and I'm not at all sure if Brother Arkady is prepared to risk anything. But of course the ironic thing is that those same damned peasants won't thank me – won't ever know of my existence. So there they'll be, all nice and cosy and smiling in their comfortable cottages and sending eggs up to Arkady in his big house; and Bazarov will be feeding the worms in some unmarked grave in the wilderness.

ARKADY: I don't know what your point is.

44

BAZAROV: That life is ridiculous and he doesn't know that it is.

ARKADY: And your life?

BAZAROV: Equally ridiculous. Maybe more ridiculous. But I'm aware that it is.

ARKADY: I'm going out for a walk.

BAZAROV: To be in good shape for the revolution or for Anna Sergeyevna?

ARKADY: If I stay we'll fight, Bazarov.

BAZAROV: Then by all means stay. Let's have a fight, Arkady. A fight between us is long overdue.

ARKADY: (*Flushed with anger*) I'm fond of you, Bazarov. But there are times when I find your arrogance very hard to take. Only Bazarov has the capacity for real sacrifice. Only Bazarov is a fully authentic revolutionary. Only Bazarov has the courage and the clarity of purpose to live outside ordinary society, without attachments, beyond the consolation of the emotions.

BAZAROV: Yes, I have that courage. Have you?

ARKADY: I'm not as cleansed as you, Bazarov. I like being with people I'm fond of. I even love some people – if you know what that means.

BAZAROV: What what means?

ARKADY: Love – loving – do you know what loving means? (*Pause.*)

BAZAROV: Yes, I know what loving means, Arkady. I love my mother. I love her very much. And I love my father very much. I don't think there are two better people in the whole of Russia.

ARKADY: You don't behave like that.

BAZAROV: How do you expect me to behave? Kiss them? Hug them? Paw over them? You're talking like an idiot. Uncle Pavel would be proud of you.

ARKADY: What did you call Uncle Pavel?

BAZAROV: An idiot. The Tailor's Dummy is an idiot.

ARKADY: Bazarov, I'm warning you—

BAZAROV: It's interesting, you know, how deep-seated domestic attachments can be. Six weeks ago – a month ago you were preaching the dismantling of the whole apparatus of state,

45

the social order, family life. But the moment I say your
Uncle Pavel is an idiot, you revert to the old cultural
stereotype. We're witnessing the death of a Nihilist and the
birth – no, the rebirth of a very nice liberal gentleman.
(ARKADY *goes rapidly and in sudden fury towards* BAZAROV.
He is almost certainly going to strike him when the door opens and
VASSILY *puts his head in. He speaks softly and is very*
embarrassed.)

VASSILY: There's something I – may I come in? – there's
something I want to talk about to both of you.
(*He comes in and closes the door behind him.*)
You're sure I'm not intruding?

ARKADY: No, not at all.

VASSILY: Well. Before we eat this evening, a local priest, Father
Alexei, is going to call on us. At your mother's request. She's
a very devout woman, as you know, Yevgeny. Unlike
myself, as you know, too. And the purpose of his visit is to –
to – to gather the family around – your mother, myself in all
probability, Yevgeny if he chooses, Arkady if he chooses –
you'd be most welcome – to gather us all around in one large
domestic circle and – and – well, really to offer up some
prayers of thanksgiving for your arrival home. A *Te Deum,*
Laudamus. 'We praise Thee, Lord'. The little informal
service will be held in my study – hence the new curtains. If
you like to attend, please do. I can't tell you how grateful
your mother would be if you did. But if you don't – and
that's an attitude I'd respect, I certainly would – then – then
– then don't. And we'll all meet for our celebratory dinner at
seven. With champagne. And that's it. All right?

BAZAROV: Yes. I'll be at the service, Father.

VASSILY: (*Delighted and relieved*) You will?!

BAZAROV: Why not. You and Mother would like me to be there.

VASSILY: Like you to?! We would—

BAZAROV: So I'll be there.

VASSILY: This is – this is just – just magnificent! Thank you,
Yevgeny. Thank you from the bottom of my heart. You have
no idea how much I appreciate that – how thrilled your
mother will be!

BAZAROV: Not at all. (*To* ARKADY.) You'll join us, won't you? But if you'd prefer not to—

ARKADY: I'll join you of course. And sorry for losing my temper just now, Bazarov. I mean that.
(BAZAROV *catches his hand.*)

BAZAROV: We were both a bit hasty. But I don't withdraw anything I said.
(ARINA *enters.*)

ARINA: Vassily, are you going to help me or are you not?

VASSILY: Arina! Good news! Great news!

BAZAROV: I'm just telling Father I'd be happy to attend the *Te Deum* service, Mother.

ARINA: Vassily?

VASSILY: Yes.

BAZAROV: It's this evening, isn't it?

VASSILY: Before we eat.

BAZAROV: Fine. As long as it's today some time. You see I'm leaving first thing in the morning.

ARINA: Leaving?

BAZAROV: Yes. I've exams in September and I've a lot of work to catch up with.

ARINA: But, son, you've only just arrived.

VASSILY: And you can study here, can't you? Amn't I right, my pet? My study is—

BAZAROV: My books are all at Arkady's home. I'll work there – if they will allow me. If they don't, I'll go back to Petersburg. But I'll come and see you for a night or two before next term begins. That's a solemn promise. Well. What time do you expect Father Alexei to arrive? When do we all sing the *Te Deum* together?
(*Quick black.*)

47

ACT TWO

SCENE I

Late August. Just before noon. Scene as in Act One.

ANNA SERGEYEVNA *and* NIKOLAI *have spent the morning looking at accounts and touring the Kirsanov estate. They have just returned. She is alone on stage, sitting at a table, examining estate maps and accounts with a quick and efficient eye.* BAZAROV *enters. He is looking for* ANNA *but when he sees her he pretends to be surprised. He is very tense.*

BAZAROV: Ah. So you're back.

ANNA: Yes.

BAZAROV: The grand tour's over?

ANNA: Yes.

BAZAROV: It didn't take you long.

ANNA: A few hours.

BAZAROV: Nice day for it.

ANNA: Lovely.

BAZAROV: Beautiful.

> (*Pause.*)
>
> I think I left a book out here somewhere . . . (*He looks around.*)
>
> Probably in the living-room.

ANNA: (*Just as he is about to exit*) How are the studies going?

BAZAROV: Well. No, not well.

ANNA: When do the exams begin?

BAZAROV: Early September. I didn't hear you come back.

ANNA: Oh, we're back about half an hour.

BAZAROV: Really?

ANNA: Yes. Maybe an hour.

BAZAROV: I didn't hear you. Well, you couldn't have chosen a better day.

ANNA: Lovely.

BAZAROV: Beautiful. (*Pause. Then he moves beside her and speaks softly and with intensity.*) We've got to have a talk before you leave, Anna. Last Wednesday in your house you said

48

something I've thought a lot about—
(*He breaks off because* NIKOLAI *enters with another bundle of estate maps.*)

NIKOLAI: Leave a thing out of your hand for five minutes in this house and somebody's sure to lift it. D'you know where they were? In the pantry! Maps in the pantry! Bats in the belfry! Ha-ha! (*Seeing* BAZAROV.) Do you know where Arkady is, Yevgeny?

BAZAROV: Yes; he's gone for a swim with Katya.

NIKOLAI: I'm glad Master Arkady's enjoying himself. He ought to have been with Anna and me all morning. This is all going to be his one day and the sooner he masters the very complicated business of running an estate – (*He drops one of the maps. Picks it up quickly.*) – firmly and efficiently, the better. Now let's organize our lives.
(*He sits at the table beside* ANNA. BAZAROV *goes off.* ANNA *watches him go.*)
We had got the length of (*map.*) number four. Where's five? – five? – five? – here we are. (*He spreads the fifth map across the table.*) Now. That's where we crossed the river. And somewhere about here – yes, there it is – that's the old well. Remember? – I pointed it out to you. (*Aware that* ANNA *is not listening.*) Are sure you're not exhausted?

ANNA: Not a bit.

NIKOLAI: Some tea? Coffee? Perhaps a glass of – ?

ANNA: I'm quite fresh. (*Concentrating fully.*) Let's carry on.

NIKOLAI: This is a tremendous help to me, Anna. I can't tell you how grateful I am. Now. We drove along that road there and that's the area that is under wheat. The estate manager's cottage would be about here; Adam's house.

ANNA: And that's where the new threshing machine is sunk in the quagmire.

NIKOLAI: Yes.

ANNA: But that's clearly marked as a swamp ground.

NIKOLAI: Yes, it is, isn't it?

ANNA: Why didn't Adam take all the heavy machinery in from the far side?

NIKOLAI: I suppose he just – just took the short-cut.

ANNA: But he must have known he couldn't get across that swamp.

NIKOLAI: Do you think I should abandon it – the thresher?

ANNA: When your tenants have finished stripping it there won't be much of a thresher left.

NIKOLAI: That means I've lost the entire wheat crop.

ANNA: Where's the map of the land east of the river?

NIKOLAI: Here we are. These buildings are my new cheese and yogurt plant. I'm afraid I spent a great deal of money on those buildings. It hasn't been exactly an unqualified success, that plant.

ANNA: Did you sell any cheese at all last year?

NIKOLAI: Not a lot. Very little. None.

ANNA: Yogurt?

NIKOLAI: A few cases. But the cheese didn't go to loss. The poorer peasants were very grateful for it when—

ANNA: What map is that?

NIKOLAI: The stables – paddock – the area behind the house here—

ANNA: No, don't open it. I know that area.

(*She checks some detail in an account book. He waits. Pause.*)

NIKOLAI: The Kirsanov estate; all five thousand acres of it. A bit of a mess, isn't it? What do you advise?

ANNA: Right. We're now in the last week of August. What I'll do is this. My crops are ready for harvesting. With a bit of organization I may be able to begin next Monday. That means that in two weeks' time all my machinery will be available. It will take – say – two days to transport it over here. So you must be ready to start the moment it arrives otherwise your wheat and corn and oats will have become too heavy and the thresher won't lift them.

NIKOLAI: But I can't possibly—

ANNA: I want to have another look at your cheese and yogurt accounts for the past year.

NIKOLAI: Of course. Piotr! Piotr!

ANNA: No, no; not now. Later. But from the quick look I had this morning it seems to me that the best thing you can do at this stage is cut your losses and close the dairy plant down.

NIKOLAI: My new plant? But it's only—

ANNA: I know you've spent a lot of money on the buildings but I think you can use them more profitably to store your wheat and oats and hay. You need more storage space anyway.

NIKOLAI: You're right.

ANNA: And finally you've got to sack that estate manager – what's his name? – Adam.

NIKOLAI: Sack my Adam?! Oh Anna, I'm afraid that's something I just couldn't—

ANNA: At best he's incompetent. And I suspect he may be corrupt. According to these records fifty foals were born last year and yet I counted only twelve yearlings this morning in the paddock.

NIKOLAI: There's an explanation for that. Apparently last winter wolves got into the enclosure and—

ANNA: That's his story. I've talked to Prokofyich. He says there have been no wolves around here for almost twenty years. You cannot run an estate this size unless you have a manager who is both competent and trustworthy.

(PIOTR *enters, as usual breathless with haste and a bogus eagerness to serve.*)

PIOTR: You wanted me, sir?

NIKOLAI: Yes, Piotr?

PIOTR: You called me, sir.

NIKOLAI: I did?

PIOTR: No question about it, sir. I heard you myself.

NIKOLAI: I'm sure I did, Piotr. And I'm sure you pretended you didn't. (*To* ANNA.) Piotr's hearing is erratic.

PIOTR: That's unfair, sir. With the deepest respect, sir, that's a bit unfair.

NIKOLAI: I apologize, Piotr. Your hearing is perfect.

PIOTR: I was carrying logs into the kitchen, sir. The moment I heard you I dropped everything.

NIKOLAI: Very well, Piotr. I'm sure you did. Anyhow, I don't want you now. Here – take all this stuff with you. You know where to leave it.

PIOTR: I certainly do, sir. Leave it to Piotr, the man in the gap. (*He takes the maps and account books and exits.*)

NIKOLAI: The man in the gap! I don't know where he gets these expressions. Well. That's a splendid morning's work. Thank you again.

ANNA: I hope it's some help.

NIKOLAI: I really feel ashamed of – of – of my stewardship. I'm not trying to make excuses for myself but the whole place fell into my lap the year I graduated. I was the same age as Arkady is now. I knew nothing at all about the land . . . Anyhow. Invaluable. I do mean that.

(*To* BAZAROV *who has entered as before.*)

Ah, Yevgeny, taking a break from the books, eh? (*To* ANNA.) I keep telling him – he studies too much. Excellent. Splendid. I must tell Pavel about my plans. (*To* BAZAROV.) Anna Sergeyevna has clarified my thinking wonderfully. I'm going to close down the cheese and yogurt plant and I'm going to get rid of Adam, the estate manager. He is neither competent nor trustworthy. I'll be back shortly.

(*He goes off.* BAZAROV *is as awkward and ill at ease as before. Pause.*)

ANNA: I don't think I clarified his thinking at all. (*Pause.*) He sounds full of purpose now but I wouldn't be surprised if some of the resolution is gone before he talks to Pavel. (*Pause.*) He thinks that his responsibilities ended when he gave the estate to the peasants to farm.

BAZAROV: I want to talk to you about a conversation you and I had last Wednesday at your house.

ANNA: Last Wednesday?

BAZAROV: It was just before dinner. We were sitting together in the conservatory. Somebody was playing a guitar in the distance. Katya's pup was lying between us and there was a circle of moisture where his nose rested on the tiled floor. You said I should offer him my handkerchief and I laughed very heartily because it sounded very, very funny . . . at that moment.

(DUNYASHA *appears briefly to do some housekeeping and exits immediately.*)

ANNA: For no reason at all that maid annoys me intensely.

BAZAROV: You were wearing a pale blue dress with a white collar and white lace cuffs. Anyhow Katya and Arkady joined us at that point when I was just about to explain what I had meant a short time before when I had said that it seemed to me that we both appeared to act on the assumption that we talked to one another across some very wide chasm that seemed to separate us even though neither of us knew why that chasm was there, if indeed it was there; but because it seemed to both of us that it was, we behaved towards one another with a certain kind of formality that was more appropriate to people who had only just met . . . Probably none of this makes much sense to you. You probably don't remember any of it – do you?

ANNA: Yes, I do.

BAZAROV: Do you?

ANNA: Bits . . . fragments . . . more your intensity than what you said . . .

BAZAROV: It was a conversation of some importance to me and I'd just like to summarize it briefly – very briefly – if I may, and to say what I intended to say then if Katya and Arkady hadn't joined us and interrupted us . . . me . . .

ANNA: Katya and Arkady are having a long swim, aren't they?

BAZAROV: We were talking about relationships. We were talking about happiness. You said that for you happiness always seemed to be just that one step beyond your reach but that you still believed that some day you would grasp it.

You said we had a lot in common; that you had been poor, too, and that you had been ambitious.

You asked me what would become of me. I said I would probably end up a country doctor somewhere in the back of beyond and you said I didn't believe that for a minute but that I wasn't prepared to tell you what I really thought.

You said you believed you could talk truthfully and openly about how you felt about things. I said I couldn't do that. You asked me why not. I said I always found it difficult to express exactly how I felt but that when I was with you I found it – found it even more difficult.

And that's how the issue of a chasm between us came up. And how that chasm inhibited us – well, inhibited me.

Because at the point when Katya and Arkady joined us, I was about to say that that chasm had prevented me from saying to you what I have wanted to say to you for weeks, what I have wanted to say to you ever since that very first day when we met here away back last May just after I had come from Petersburg – that I'm mad about you, Anna Sergeyevna, hopelessly, insanely, passionately, extravagantly, madly in love with you.

ANNA: Oh Yevgeny, Yevgeny—

BAZAROV: Yes, I am, I am. You know I am. I can't eat. I can't sleep. I can't study. I'm obsessed with you. I'm besotted by you. Let me kiss you, Anna. Please. Please let me kiss you.
(*He takes her in his arms and kisses her. She does not free herself immediately. Then suddenly she pushes him away roughly.*)

ANNA: Yevgeny! Please! Oh, my God! You shouldn't have done that.

BAZAROV: Yes-yes-yes.

ANNA: No, you shouldn't. You've misunderstood the whole situation. You've misread the whole thing.

BAZAROV: No, I haven't, Anna. And you wanted me to kiss you. Admit that.

ANNA: Yes, you have, Yevgeny. Oh, yes, you have. Misread it totally. Oh, my God . . .
(*She rushes into the house.*)

BAZAROV: Anna – ! Anna, please – !
(*But she is gone. He is distraught. He does not know whether to run after her or to run away. Then he hears* KATYA *and* ARKADY *approach – they are laughing and calling to one another. He cannot escape that way. The only other hiding place is the gazebo. He rushes to it, sits down, pulls a book from his pocket, opens it at random and pretends to be immersed in it.*)

ARKADY: (*Off*) Give that shoe back to me!

KATYA: (*Off*) I will not!

ARKADY: (*Off*) Katya, I'm warning you.

KATYA: (*Off*) Come and get it yourself.
(*She runs on laughing; her hair wet, her towel flying, his shoe in her hand.*)
O my God!

(*She looks round frantically for somewhere to hide the shoe. She sees* BAZAROV *in the gazebo.*)

I've got his shoe! He's going mad! Can I hide it here?

ARKADY: (*Off*) Katya! Katya?

(*She approaches* BAZAROV *and realizes at once that something is amiss. Pause.*)

KATYA: (*Quietly, seriously*) Yevgeny? Are you all right, Yevgeny?

ARKADY: (*Off*) Katya! Where are you?

(*She gazes at him, hunched, tense, behind his book. She reaches out to touch him.*)

KATYA: Yevgeny?

ARKADY: You're for it, madam – I'm telling you!

(ARKADY *is just outside. She withdraws her hand and runs out of the gazebo.*)

KATYA: I've hidden it in the gazebo, Arkady!

(*She runs into the living-room and hides behind a door.* ARKADY *enters, limping; a limp similar to his father's.*)

ARKADY: I'm warning you, girl! You've crippled me – that's what you've done! (*To himself.*) The gazebo . . .

(*He goes to the gazebo and searches it. As he does:*)

Was Katya here, Bazarov? Where did she hide my shoe? I'm going to kill that girl!

KATYA: (*Appearing on the veranda*) Cold, Arkady. Very cold. Getting colder, much colder.

ARKADY: Come on, Katya! Where is it? Where is it? My feet are wrecked with bloody thorns!

KATYA: (*Holding up a shoe*) This isn't yours, is it?

(*She laughs and disappears into the living-room. He runs/hops after her. As he does:*)

ARKADY: You told me lies! You misled me! Just you wait there, madam! I'm going to twist your neck! Katya! Katya! Wait there! Wait!

(*He disappears into the living-room. Their laughter dies away.* BAZAROV *closes his book. He sits with his eyes shut tight, his shoulders tensed and hunched, his whole body rigid and anguished.* FENICHKA *enters carrying a large bunch of roses she has just cut. Just before she enters the house she glances over at the gazebo, thinks she sees somebody, looks again and recognizes*

55

BAZAROV. *She approaches slowly and studies him for a few seconds before she speaks to him. She speaks softly.*)

FENICHKA: Yevgeny, is there something wrong?
(*He opens his eyes suddenly. He is startled.*)

BAZAROV: Hello? – yes? – yes?

FENICHKA: Are you all right, Yevgeny? Is something the matter?
(*He flashes a smile at her and speaks with excessive enthusiasm, almost in panic.*)

BAZAROV: Fenichka! It's you! How are you? I'm glad to see you – I'm delighted to see you! Yes, yes, I'm fine, I'm fine, I'm really fine, Fenichka. I mean that – I really do – honestly. It's all over and I'm still alive. In fact I'm perfectly well. But how are you? I haven't seen you for days and days and I've missed you. Where have you been hiding?

FENICHKA: You're the one who has been hiding – upstairs reading those books of yours.

BAZAROV: Sit down beside me. Talk to me.
(*She sits beside him.*)

FENICHKA: What about?

BAZAROV: It doesn't matter. About chasms and relationships and happiness – about your healing presence in this disturbed house – about those tranquil roses. They're beautiful roses.
(*Sound of* NIKOLAI *playing the cello in the distance: Beethoven's* Romance *for violin and orchestra in G-major, Op. 40.*)

FENICHKA: They're past their best. But Nikolai likes to have flowers on the dining-room table.

BAZAROV: Nikolai is blessed. That's a strange word for me to use – blessed. Six months ago I would have said the word had no meaning. But it has – it describes the condition of someone, anyone, to whom the beautiful Fenichka turns her open face and on whom she smiles. Yes, I have missed you. It's not that we ever talk – this is probably the first time we've ever been alone together – but I'm always aware of your presence in the house, even when you're not there. I think it's because you generate goodness. That's another strange word for me.

And suddenly it has meaning, too. You're equipping me
with a new vocabulary, Fenichka!

FENICHKA: Will you stop talking like that, Yevgeny! I don't
understand a word you're saying!

BAZAROV: Are you happy, Fenichka? I hope you are. Are you?
(*He takes her hand in his.* PAVEL *enters from the living-room.
He is engrossed in a book. He pauses on the veranda and then
moves slowly downstage.*)

FENICHKA: I don't think about things like that.

BAZAROV: Then you are.

FENICHKA: I'm young. I have my health. I have Mitya.

BAZAROV: And you have Nikolai.
(*She withdraws her hand.*)

FENICHKA: Nikolai is a kind man.

BAZAROV: Yes, he is. Do you love him?

FENICHKA: Do you remember those drops you gave me for
Mitya? Three days ago – remember? – he was vomiting – you
thought he had eaten something. Well, they worked
miracles. He was as right as rain in a couple of hours.

BAZAROV: I'm glad of that. So now you must pay me.
(FENICHKA *is unsure and embarrassed.*)

FENICHKA: I – ?

BAZAROV: Doctors have to be paid, don't they? Doctors are
notoriously greedy people, aren't they?

FENICHKA: You're right, Yevgeny. I'm sorry. I'll speak to
Nikolai today and he'll—

BAZAROV: No, no, no, no, no, no, Fenichka. I don't want
money. It's not mere money I want. I want something
personal – from you.

FENICHKA: What is that?

BAZAROV: Guess.

FENICHKA: I'm no good at guessing, Yevgeny.

BAZAROV: All right. I'll tell you what I want from you. I
want . . . one of those roses.
(*The cello music stops.
She laughs with relief. He laughs with her.*)

FENICHKA: What colour would you like, sir?

BAZAROV: A red one. A small red one, Fenichka Fedosya.

FENICHKA: There you are, Yevgeny Vassilyich – one small red rose.
(Between them they drop it. Together they stoop down to pick it up. Their hands meet on the ground. They laugh briefly and then stop. They look at one another. He kisses her on the lips. PAVEL *is now downstage and happens to look across at them at the moment they kiss.* FENICHKA *looks over* BAZAROV's *shoulder and sees* PAVEL *watching.)*

PAVEL: So this is how Nihilists betray hospitality.

FENICHKA: *(Jumps to her feet and moves towards* PAVEL) There is nothing, Pavel Petrovich – I swear before God – there is nothing at all—
(She rushes off.)

BAZAROV: Fenichka, your flowers—
(He begins to pick them up.)

PAVEL: What are your views on duelling, Monsieur Bazarov?

BAZAROV: Sorry?

PAVEL: I said what are your views on duelling?

BAZAROV: I have no 'views' on duelling.

PAVEL: Would you accept that it is a method by which gentlemen can settle their differences?

BAZAROV: I think it's just another method of killing – or being killed.

PAVEL: But if you were insulted you would demand satisfaction?

BAZAROV: I don't know. Maybe. I suppose so.

PAVEL: Excellent.
*(*BAZAROV *has now gathered the scattered flowers and for the first time faces* PAVEL.)*

BAZAROV: What's this all about?

PAVEL: I wish to fight you.
*(*BAZAROV *now realizes that* PAVEL *is deadly serious.)*

BAZAROV: A duel? You want to fight a duel with me?!

PAVEL: Tomorrow morning at six.

BAZAROV: You're not serious!

PAVEL: Behind the birch plantation.

BAZAROV: But – but – but why would you want to fight with me?

PAVEL: It is sufficient for you to know that I despise you – indeed, I detest you.

58

BAZAROV: But that's no reason to *fight*, Pavel Petrovich!
 (PAVEL *raises his walking-stick as if to strike* BAZAROV.)
PAVEL: If you wish I'll give you a more immediate reason.
BAZAROV: You're serious! Good God, the man's serious!
PAVEL: We will use pistols at a distance of ten paces.
BAZAROV: I can't shoot.
PAVEL: Every gentleman can shoot.
BAZAROV: I haven't got a pistol.
PAVEL: We will use my pistols.
BAZAROV: I'm not taking part in this, Pavel.
PAVEL: We will dispense with seconds. I'll get Piotr to act as witness.
BAZAROV: Why are you doing this? What is this all – ?
PAVEL: Nobody else need be involved. Tomorrow morning at six, then.
BAZAROV: Good God Almighty! What in Christ's name is the—
 (*He stops suddenly because he suddenly knows the reason for the challenge.*)
 You're jealous, Pavel Petrovich! You saw me kissing Fenichka and you thought—
PAVEL: Behind the birch plantation. Be there.
 (*He moves away.*
 NIKOLAI *appears on the veranda. Neither* PAVEL *nor* BAZAROV *sees him nor hears him.*)
NIKOLAI: Ah, Pavel. We should both go and have a word with—
BAZAROV: That's it! Of course! You're jealous, Pavel Petrovich! You're jealous because you're in love with Fenichka! O my God! (*Remembering the duel.*) O my God . . .
 (NIKOLAI *retreats into the living-room.* BAZAROV *drops into a seat.*)

SCENE 2

The following morning.

DUNYASHA is gathering up dishes that are on a table downstage left close to the gazebo. She has only recently stopped crying – her face is red and she is snivelling.

PROKOFYICH enters from the living-room. He is carrying a case which he leaves upstage left. When DUNYASHA sees the case she sobs again.

PROKOFYICH: Get a move on, Dunyasha. Don't spend all morning picking up a few dishes.

DUNYASHA: (*Sotto voce*) Shut up, you old get.

PROKOFYICH: I'm talking to you, miss.

DUNYASHA: (*Sotto voce*) Bugger off.

PROKOFYICH: The guest room is empty – at last. Change the sheets and the pillowcases and sweep the place out thoroughly.

DUNYASHA: Have I your permission to finish this job first, Prokofyich, sir?

PROKOFYICH: We'll do without your lip, missy. Then take the mattress and the floor mats and leave them out in the sun for the rest of the day. Maybe they should be fumigated.

(*To* PIOTR *who has entered with another case.*)

Come on, boy! Move! Move! Move! The sooner this house gets back to normal the better.

(*PROKOFYICH goes back into the house. PIOTR leaves his case beside the first and goes downstage to join DUNYASHA. All the assurance, all the perkiness is gone. He is thoroughly wretched. He has to tell his story to somebody. DUNYASHA does not want to listen – she has her own grief. He holds out his hands. They are trembling.*)

PIOTR: Look, Dunyasha – look – look – I can't stop them – look. And my whole body feels as if it's trembling, too. Give me your hand – put it there (*his heart*) – it's galloping like a bloody horse; and about every ten minutes or so it stops – dead.

60

(*She ignores him and continues working and snivelling.*)

DUNYASHA: Get out of my road, will you!

PIOTR: What – what – what's that?

DUNYASHA: You're in my way, Piotr!

PIOTR: (*Almost in tears*) I don't hear a word you're saying,
     Dunyasha. As true as God's above. I'm as deaf as a post.

DUNYASHA: So you've told me.

PIOTR: What happened was this—

DUNYASHA: I don't want to hear about it.

PIOTR: Yevgeny was about there and I was about here and the
     Tailor's Dummy was about there – (*Trembling hand.*) – look!
     – didn't I tell you – there! – there! – there! God, the sight of
     this is going to break my mammy's heart. Anyway, Yevgeny
     and the Tailor's Dummy had their backs to one another; and
     just when they were about to turn to face each other,
     Yevgeny called me to him and he whispered, 'How do you
     cock a gun, Piotr?' and the sweat's standing out on his
     forehead and he's holding the gun like this and his eyes are
     half-shut and he's facing the other way. 'How do you cock a
     gun?' – for Christ's sake! And I'm standing as close to him as
     I am to you now and I reach over to pull the hammer back
     and he sort of turns towards me and whatever messing we're
     both at, suddenly, suddenly there's this huge explosion right
     beside my cheek—

PROKOFYICH: (*On the veranda*) Piotr!

PIOTR: —and I thought, my God, I thought, he's blown my head
     off—

DUNYASHA: You're wanted, Piotr.

PIOTR: —because I fell to the ground and I could hear nothing
     and see nothing and feel nothing. And then the smoke
     cleared and there, lying across a fallen birch tree, there's—
     (PROKOFYICH *has come up behind* PIOTR *and now grips him
     by the arm.*)

PROKOFYICH: Are you a guest here, boy?

PIOTR: What's that, Prokofyich? I think my drums are ruptured.

PROKOFYICH: (*Very loudly into his face*) Can you hear me now,
     Piotr?

PIOTR: Shouting's no help, Prokofyich.

61

PROKOFYICH: If you don't get back to work at once – at once! – I'll rupture your head, Piotr. Harness the carriage. Bring it round to the back. Now! (*He pushes* PIOTR *roughly.* PIOTR *goes off left.* PROKOFYICH *now turns to* DUNYASHA. *She is wiping the surface of the table.*) That's all right. Leave it now. No need to make a meal of it. Get upstairs and clean out that guest-room. (*As he is about to go off left:*)

DUNYASHA: I'm thinking of leaving, Prokofyich.

PROKOFYICH: (*Without hesitating*) Don't think about it, miss. Just leave.

DUNYASHA: Well, if I do, I won't do it just because you would want me to do it. If I do it, I'll do it because I want to . . . (*But he has already gone. She wipes her nose, lifts her tray and goes towards the house.*

Just as she approaches the veranda steps, ARKADY *and* PAVEL *and* NIKOLAI *come out of the living-room.* PAVEL *is very pale and his arm is in a sling.*

ARKADY *comes first, walking backwards.* NIKOLAI *holds* PAVEL'*s 'good' arm even though* PAVEL *has a walking-stick.* ARKADY *and* NIKOLAI *fuss over him as if he were very ill. He is barely able to keep his temper.*)

ARKADY: Careful, Uncle Pavel, careful.

NIKOLAI: Watch that step.

ARKADY: Take it slowly. There's no rush.

NIKOLAI: (*To* DUNYASHA) Watch, girl. Out of the way.

ARKADY: Get a cushion, Dunyasha. Two cushions. (*She goes into the house.*)

NIKOLAI: Let me take that stick, Pavel, and you can hold on to my arm.

ARKADY: (*Preparing a seat*) Here we are, Uncle Pavel.

NIKOLAI: Turn it round. He doesn't like the direct sun. Splendid. Now get something for his feet.

PAVEL: (*Groans*) O my God . . .

NIKOLAI: (*Misunderstanding the groan*) I know you're in pain. Hang on for another second. That's it now, Pavel – here we are. Sink back into that – gently – gently – that's it – lovely. Can you lean forward a little? (*He slips a cushion behind*

62

PAVEL.) Excellent.
(*At the same time* ARKADY *puts the second cushion, which*
DUNYASHA *has brought, on a stool and slips the stool under*
PAVEL's *feet.*)
Thank you, Arkady. Now we're more comfortable, aren't we?
(DUNYASHA *leaves.*)

ARKADY: Should I get a lower stool?

NIKOLAI: I think that's about right. (*To* PAVEL.) That bandage
isn't too tight, is it?

ARKADY: He lost a lot of blood, you know.

NIKOLAI: As long as the fingers are free to—

PAVEL: (*Almost a shout*) Please! (*Now softly and controlled.*) *S'il*
vous plaît. I got a superficial cut. I lost a few drops of blood. I
am properly bandaged. I am in no pain.

NIKOLAI: Pavel, you have been through a shocking—

PAVEL: I am perfectly well and perfectly comfortable, thank you
very much, and I would be very grateful if both of you would
leave me alone now. There's a green-backed book sitting on
the couch in the conservatory, Arkady. Would you bring it
to me?
(ARKADY *goes into the house. Pause.*)
I owe you an apology, Nikolai. I am sorry to have caused all
this . . . upset. I apologize. I won't mention it again.
(*Pause.* PAVEL *puts perfume on his hands.*)
If anybody's going into town today, I'd be grateful if they'd
get me some eau-de-Cologne.
(*Pause.*)
I overheard young Katya talking to her sister yesterday
afternoon. She referred to me as 'beau-de-Cologne'. Not
bad, I thought. I like that little lady. Spirited.
(*Pause.*)
And I understand Bazarov is leaving us.

NIKOLAI: Why did you have the duel with him, Pavel?

PAVEL: It was my fault entirely.

NIKOLAI: What did you fight about?

PAVEL: We had a political disagreement.

NIKOLAI: What about?

PAVEL: I don't wish to discuss it further, Nikolai.

63

NIKOLAI: I would like you to tell me exactly what the disagreement was about, Pavel.

(ARKADY *returns with the book*.)

ARKADY: *The Castles of Athlin and Dunbayne* – is this it?

PAVEL: Set in Scotland. The wonderful Mrs Ann Ward Radcliffe. She's charming – she understands nothing.

ARKADY: There's something I'd like to say, Uncle Pavel. Formally. In my father's presence.

PAVEL: Oh dear – a manifesto.

ARKADY: Because I brought Bazarov to this house, I feel at least partly responsible for whatever happened this morning – I know now I shouldn't have brought him here in the first place but—

NIKOLAI: Nonsense, Arkady. This is your home.

ARKADY: I'm trying to be rational and fair, Father. Our friendship was very important to me. It still is. So I want to be fair to that friendship and at the same time I don't want to judge anybody quickly or rashly. So I'm afraid I must ask you, Uncle Pavel, to tell me exactly, if you would, please, exactly what—

PAVEL: Exactly – exactly – exactly! Why this sudden passion for exactitude? Very well. Let's get the damned thing said once and for all. But first I want a promise from you both that what I am going to tell you will not be repeated by either of you to anybody. Do I have that assurance?

(*They both nod*.)

ARKADY: Of course you do.

PAVEL: Well. Monsieur Bazarov and I were talking about English politicians. About Sir Robert Peel, to be exact, and his family background. I said Peel's father was a wealthy land-owner. Bazarov said he was a cotton manufacturer. I've looked it up since. I was wrong. Bazarov was in the right. Not that that matters – the issue itself was trivial. But one word, as they say, borrowed another. Tempers, as they say, too, flared. In a moment of irrationality I challenged him to a duel. He was astonished – naturally. And he met me this morning merely to flatter my pathetic pride. All in all he behaved admirably. His gun went off accidentally. I fired

64

into the air. I have acquired some respect for Monsieur Bazarov. Some modest respect. (*Pause.*) I will never mention that episode ever again. (*Pause.*) Now will somebody please tell me why Prokofyich is stumping about the house like an enraged beast?

ARKADY: He disliked Bazarov from the beginning. Now he believes he has a reason to hate him.

PAVEL: Isn't he a loyal soul? Life must be very simple for him. (PIOTR *enters from the left, exactly as we saw him at the beginning of the scene.*)

PIOTR: The carriage is waiting in the yard, sir. (*Immediately after he makes his announcement* PIOTR *turns and goes off left.*)

NIKOLAI: Thank you, Piotr. Oh, Piotr – my straw hat's in the hall. Would you bring it to—Piotr! Piotr! My God, did you see that! He ignored me! The insolent pup ignored me! Oh-ho, Master Piotr is certainly going to go. There are going to be changes about here. I'm not going to be insulted in my own house by a servant or by anybody else.

PAVEL: I don't think he heard you, Nikolai.

NIKOLAI: (*Violently*) That's a damned lie! And you know that's a damned lie! The bastard never hears me! Never! Never! I'm sick of him never hearing me! Sick to death of it! (*Quickly recovering.*) Forgive me . . . I'm sorry . . . That was unpardonable . . . Forgive me . . . I think I'll play the cello for a while . . . The cello, I find, is very . . . healing . . . (*He goes into the house.* ARKADY *is astonished at the outburst.* PAVEL *has some idea why it happened.*)

PAVEL: Good Lord. What was that all about?

ARKADY: He never really warmed to Bazarov either.

PAVEL: Perhaps.

ARKADY: I know Bazarov likes him very much but he can't show affection easily.

PAVEL: What are his plans?

ARKADY: He intended going to Petersburg to study. But when he was packing this morning he got a message that there's a typhus epidemic in his home province; so he's going there first to help his father out.

PAVEL: Ah. Very worthy. I'm thinking of moving out myself.

ARKADY: What do you mean?

PAVEL: Just going away. Leaving.

ARKADY: Where to?

PAVEL: Germany. France. England. Maybe Scotland! Perhaps I should buy the castle of Dunbayne?

ARKADY: You don't mean leaving for good, Uncle Pavel, do you?!

PAVEL: We'll see. But certainly not until after the harvest is saved. They couldn't save the hay without my muscle, could they? Ah, Monsieur Bazarov. I hear you're going home?

(BAZAROV *enters left with a book in his hand. He is dressed for travelling. He leaves his jacket beside his cases and comes down to* ARKADY *and* PAVEL.

This is now a fully mature young man – neither in his clothes nor in his demeanour is there any trace of the student. His manner is brisk, efficient, almost icy.)

BAZAROV: How is the arm?

PAVEL: Fine, thank you. You dressed it well.

BAZAROV: Take the bandage off after three days and let the fresh air at the wound.

(*The sound of* NIKOLAI *playing the cello:* Romance *in F-Major, Op. 50.*)

PAVEL: Le malade n'est pas à plaindre qui a la guérison en sa manche.

BAZAROV: I don't speak French.

PAVEL: Montaigne. It means: don't pity the sick man who—

(BAZAROV *turns abruptly away from him.*)

BAZAROV: (*To* ARKADY) I must say goodbye to your father.

(*He goes towards his cases.* ARKADY *follows him, takes his arm and speaks to him quietly, privately, in an attempt to restore the old intimacy.* PAVEL *goes off to the far side of the garden and reads.*)

ARKADY: I have a plan, Bazarov. I'll go to Petersburg at Christmas; back to the old flat; and we'll —

BAZAROV: No, you won't do that, Arkady. By Christmas you and Katya will probably be married.

(*They continue this conversation as* BAZAROV *opens a case and puts his book into it.*)

66

ARKADY: Married?! Me?! For God's sake, man, we Nihilists
don't believe in—
BAZAROV: And I'm pleased for you. She'll take you in hand and
you want to be taken in hand. You're naturally
complementary. And natural elements that complement one
another tend to create a balanced and stable unit.
ARKADY: Cut that out, Bazarov! Stop addressing me, man! This
is your old matie, Arkady, your old cook and bottle washer.
And what I'm going to do is fix a date for a big reunion.
Immediately after you finish your exams! – Mid-September!
I'll go to Petersburg. We'll get a keg of beer. We'll get all the
boys from the old cell together and—
BAZAROV: We won't be getting together again, Arkady. We both
know that. We are saying goodbye now. From your point of
view you're making all the sensible choices because
instinctively you know you're not equipped for our harsh
and bitter and lonely life.
ARKADY: Who the hell do you mean by 'our', Bazarov? I'm a
Nihilist, too, remember?
BAZAROV: When you were a student. But your heart never really
forsook the gentry and the public decencies and the
acceptable decorum. Of course you have courage and of
course you have your honest passion. But it's a gentleman's
courage and a gentleman's passion. You are concerned about
'difficult issues' but you believe they are settled by rational,
gentlemanly debate and if that doesn't work, by gentlemanly
duels. But that's not how real change, radical change is
brought about, Arkady. The world won't be remade by
discussion and mock battles at dawn. As you told your uncle
a long, long time ago we're long past the stage of social
analysis. We are now into the era of hostilities – of
scratching, hurting, biting, mauling, cutting, bruising,
spitting. You're not equipped for those indecencies. When it
would come to the bit you would retreat into well-bred
indignation and well-bred resignation. Your upbringing has
provided you with that let-out. Mine didn't. I am committed
to the last, mean, savage, glorious, shaming extreme.
ARKADY: I see.

BAZAROV: To be blunt with you, Arkady: you are not good enough for us.

ARKADY: Was it that savage, shaming side of you that frightened Anna Sergeyevna off? I shouldn't have said that. Forgive me, Bazarov.

(BAZAROV *responds as calmly and as coldly as before.*)

BAZAROV: No need to apologize. I may very well have frightened Anna Sergeyevna. But if that is what happened, I have no regrets. Miniature empires have no appeal to me. My sights are trained on a much, much larger territory.

We had a good year together, Arkady. Thank you for that.

ARKADY: Bazarov, I still think we should—

(*He stops because* FENICHKA *has come from the living-room and joins them. She has a package of sandwiches for* BAZAROV.)

FENICHKA: So you're all set.

BAZAROV: Yes.

FENICHKA: Did someone say something about a typhus epidemic?

BAZAROV: My father. He likes dramatic language. It's all probably a ruse to get me home.

FENICHKA: Well, don't take any unnecessary risks, Doctor. I made a few sandwiches for the journey. I know you like cold lamb.

BAZAROV: Thank you very much.

(*The conversation is punctuated by the awkward silences that farewells create.*)

ARKADY: Who's driving you?

BAZAROV: Prokofyich. He volunteered.

FENICHKA: You're honoured. He doesn't drive me.

BAZAROV: He's just making sure he's getting rid of me.

(*Brief laughter. Silence.*)

I must say goodbye to your father.

ARKADY: Yes.

FENICHKA: He told me he prefers playing piano duets with Katya to playing the cello by himself.

ARKADY: Yes, I think he enjoys the duets.

FENICHKA: He says Katya is as good as your mother.

ARKADY: Did he say that?

(DUNYASHA *appears at the living-room door.*)

DUNYASHA: (*Calls*) Fenichka.

FENICHKA: Yes?

(DUNYASHA *beckons.*)

What is it?

(FENICHKA *goes to* DUNYASHA.)

ARKADY: Dunyasha's suddenly very coy.

(DUNYASHA *gives the bottle of milk to* FENICHKA. *They exchange a few words.* DUNYASHA *keeps her face averted.*)

BAZAROV: (*Calls*) Goodbye, Dunyasha.

(DUNYASHA *disappears.* FENICHKA *returns.*)

FENICHKA: She has a very bad head-cold. This is a bottle of milk for the journey. She says to say goodbye.

BAZAROV: Thank her for me, will you?

FENICHKA: I will.

BAZAROV: I think she thought I wasn't sticking at the books enough: she kept bringing cups of tea up to my room. (*Silence.*)

ARKADY: He's talking about going away, too. Uncle Pavel. France. Germany. Scotland, maybe!

FENICHKA: For a holiday?

ARKADY: For good, he says.

BAZAROV: You'll have an empty house.

FENICHKA: He's not serious, is he?

ARKADY: I think he is.

FENICHKA: When is he leaving?

ARKADY: After the harvest is in. He wants to do his share of the scything.

FENICHKA: Pavel?!

ARKADY: Yes!

FENICHKA: You're joking!

ARKADY: No, I'm not. Yes, of course I am.

FENICHKA: Pavel scything! Can you imagine? Shh . . .

(*Again the brief laughter. The cello stops. Silence.* PAVEL *moves towards them.*)

PAVEL: Are the beautiful Katya and Anna joining us for dinner tonight?

ARKADY: Great! (*Recovering.*) Are they? That's news to me.

PAVEL: Am I wrong?

FENICHKA: It's tomorrow night.

ARKADY: I thought it was Sunday.

PAVEL: (*Looking straight at* FENICHKA) Ah. Then I was wrong. Yet again.

FENICHKA: They're coming straight here after church. That was the arrangement.

PAVEL: (*Still looking straight at* FENICHKA) My mistake. I get things wrong, Fenichka. Sorry.

FENICHKA: Tomorrow night.

PAVEL: I see. *Bon. Bon.*

BAZAROV: I think I should call Prokofyich.

ARKADY: (*Holding on*) Katya has finally chosen a name for her pup, Pavel.

PAVEL: Pup? What pup?

ARKADY: The borzoi pup she got from us at the beginning of the summer! She's going to call it Pavel!

(*Brief laughter.* NIKOLAI *joins them.*)

PAVEL: I suppose it's one way to be remembered?

NIKOLAI: We're all ready for departure, are we, Yevgeny? Good. Great. And Piotr's driving you, is he? Good. Excellent. (*Calls.*) Piotr!

ARKADY: Prokofyich's taking him, Father.

NIKOLAI: Prokofyich? (*Softly.*) Much better. Much more reliable. You should be in Petersburg well before night.

BAZAROV: I'm not going to Petersburg. I'm going home.

NIKOLAI: Good. Good. Excellent in fact. I'm sure your parents will be delighted to have you. Indeed. Just as we were.

BAZAROV: Thank you for all your hospitality, Nikolai Petrovich.

NIKOLAI: It was my pleasure. It was our pleasure. We'll all miss you – won't we? I'll miss all those early morning walks we had – occasionally. And Pavel will miss those – those – those stirring political discussions. And Arkady will miss the student banter. And Fenichka – Fenichka – Fenichka will miss your excellent medical advice – won't you? And—

(PROKOFYICH *appears left. Absurdly stiff-backed and formal. He stares at a point above everybody's head.*)

70

PROKOFYICH: (*Loudly*) I beg your pardon.

NIKOLAI: What is it, Prokofyich?

PROKOFYICH: The carriage is about to depart.

NIKOLAI: Yes, we know, Prokofyich. Thank you.

PROKOFYICH: I merely mention the fact in case any person
wishes to travel in it.
(*He lifts the cases and exits stiffly.*
They stare after him in astonishment and amusement. A quick,
stifled giggle from FENICHKA. *One from* ARKADY. *Then*
FENICHKA *explodes. Then they all laugh, excessively, in relief.*
BAZAROV *only smiles. He observes the happy family group from*
the outside.)

NIKOLAI: Shhh! He'll hear you.

ARKADY: He couldn't – he couldn't even look at us!

NIKOLAI: I know – I know—

ARKADY: In case any person – any person wishes to travel in it!

FENICHKA: It's going to be a – a – a –
(*She breaks down again.*)

PAVEL: A what?

FENICHKA: Can't say it.

NIKOLAI: Shhh!

ARKADY: I know what she's trying to—(*Breaks down.*)

PAVEL: A what?

FENICHKA: It's going to be a very chatty journey!
(*Again they explode. Then as suddenly the laughter dies. Silence.*)

NIKOLAI: Oh dear – oh dear – oh dear.

ARKADY: It was that eye fixed on the sky.

FENICHKA: I know. And the shoulders back.

NIKOLAI: Poor old Prokofyich. But we mean no harm, do we?
No, no; we mean no harm at all.

ARKADY: About to depart. Oh, I'm sore. Very sore.
(*Silence.*

BAZAROV *goes to* NIKOLAI.)

BAZAROV: Again, thank you for everything.

NIKOLAI: You'll come and stay with us again – perhaps.
(*They shake hands.* BAZAROV *now goes to* PAVEL.)

BAZAROV: (*Bows*) Pavel Petrovich.
(*They shake hands.*)

PAVEL: Thank you. *Adieu.*

(*BAZAROV goes to FENICHKA. He takes her hand.*)

BAZAROV: I wish you every happiness, Fenichka. Take care of yourself.

FENICHKA: You, too, Yevgeny.

(*He goes to ARKADY and holds out his hand.*)

BAZAROV: Arkady.

(*ARKADY hesitates and then impulsively embraces him.*)

ARKADY: I don't give a damn what you say! Mid-September! After the exams! That's settled. And make it two kegs.

(*He releases BAZAROV. He is crying.*)

Come on, you twisted, perverse bastard!

Clear out to hell! Move! Move!

(*He pushes BAZAROV in front of him. They exit. NIKOLAI follows them, then PAVEL.*)

He's coming, Prokofyich! Here's your passenger!

(*FENICHKA is alone on stage. She listens to the voices off. The lines overlap.*)

NIKOLAI: (*Off*) Put the bags at your feet.

ARKADY: (*Off*) Where's your jacket?

PAVEL: (*Off*) Good luck, Yevgeny.

BAZAROV: (*Off*) Thank you very much.

ARKADY: (*Off*) All set?

BAZAROV: (*Off*) I left a book somewhere.

ARKADY: (*Off*) It's in your hand. Fool.

BAZAROV: (*Off*) Thank you again.

NIKOLAI: (*Off*) Good luck with the exams.

ARKADY: (*Off*) Mid-September. That's settled.

PAVEL: (*Off*) Have a good journey.

ARKADY: (*Off*) Give my love to your father and mother.

BAZAROV: (*Off*) Goodbye.

ARKADY: (*Off*) Write me, Bazarov.

BAZAROV: (*Off*) I will.

NIKOLAI: (*Off*) Goodbye.

PAVEL: (*Off*) Goodbye.

(*A chorus of goodbyes. FENICHKA waves tentatively and says 'goodbye' quietly.*

DUNYASHA, who has been watching from the living-room, now

72

comes down and stands behind FENICHKA. FENICHKA *turns and sees her. She is sobbing helplessly.*)

DUNYASHA: All he had to do, Fenichka – all he had to do was raise his little finger and I'd have kissed his feet.

FENICHKA: Oh, Dunyasha—

DUNYASHA: Oh God, I would have, Fenichka. Just raise his little finger.

(*She throws her arms around* FENICHKA *and sobs.* FENICHKA *holds her.*)

FENICHKA: Shhh. I know, Dunyasha. I know. I know.

Early September. Afternoon. The dining-room in the Bazarov home.
VASSILY *is standing at the head of the table, always on the point of
lighting his pipe.* ARKADY *is sitting at the bottom of the table,
immobile, staring at the ground. (This is not where he sat in Act One
Scene 3.) He is scarcely aware that* VASSILY *is speaking.* VASSILY
*is smiling as fixedly as in Act One and is even more breezy and
energetic. But the energy is spurious and it is soon apparent that
occasionally he forgets what he is saying – hence the repetitions in his
speech – and that he is on the point of breakdown.*

VASSILY: Yes, yes, that was a memorable lunch. I recall every
detail of that lunch with total clarity. Oh yes, that was one of
the happiest occasions ever in this house. We'd been
expecting you for so long, you see – for years, for heaven's
sake! And now here you were, in this very room, around this
very table. And all I can say now – and I was aware of it then,
too – was that your presence alone quickened these ancient
bones again. *Omnia animat, format, alit*, as Cicero says . . .
omnia animat . . . That doesn't sound like Cicero, does
it? . . . Oh yes, that was a lunch to remember. That's the
event that furnished us with the richest and warmest
memories – that's not inaccurate, my pet, is it? . . . (*He looks
around. Realizes she is not there.*) Where had she placed us? I
was here. And she was there. And you were sitting where
you're sitting now. And Yevgeny was over there. And I have
one particularly vivid recollection. I had just told you that
story of the retired major who practises medicine 'just for
the good of the community'; and the two of you gazed at me
for a second and then suddenly collapsed with laughter; and
there you both are, spread across the table, convulsed,
unable to speak! Oh, that's a particularly vivid memory.
'Just for the good of the community.' Couldn't move.
Couldn't speak.

(TIMOFEICH *shuffles in. He seems even more decrepit than
before. He begins pottering aimlessly with the dishes on the table.*)

74

And Timofeich was looking after us as usual, weren't you, Timofeich?

TIMOFEICH: She's awake.

(VASSILY, *suddenly alert, leads* TIMOFEICH *to the side so that* ARKADY *will not hear the conversation.* ARKADY *is scarcely aware that* TIMOFEICH *is there.*)

VASSILY: Well?

TIMOFEICH: No change.

VASSILY: Did she speak?

TIMOFEICH: Not a word.

VASSILY: Is she still in bed?

TIMOFEICH: She's in the study.

VASSILY: What's she doing there?

TIMOFEICH: Sitting.

VASSILY: On the couch?

TIMOFEICH: On the swivel chair. You should comb her hair for her.

(TIMOFEICH *returns to the table.*)

VASSILY: Leave that stuff, Timofeich. And stay with her, will you?

TIMOFEICH: She can't go on without food in her. You should get her to eat.

VASSILY: (*Sudden fear*) Where's my medicine bag, Timofeich?

(TIMOFEICH *points to a high shelf where the bag is almost hidden.*)

Ah! Good man. Thank you. Thank you.

TIMOFEICH: What are you thanking me for? You hid it there yourself.

(TIMOFEICH *exits.* VASSILY *assumes the smile again and the breezy manner.*)

VASSILY: He's been a tower of strength to me, old Timofeich. I don't know what I'd have done without him.

ARKADY: How is Arina Vlassyevna?

VASSILY: She'll be with us in a while. Arina Vlassyevna is – what's the cliché? – she is as comfortable as can be expected – everything considered – considering everything. But we were discussing that lunch, weren't we? Oh, that was a memorable occasion. Do you happen to remember a boy who helped at table that day? – a very young boy? – in his bare feet? – Fedka? I have a confession to make about Fedka: Fedka wasn't a servant of ours at all. We hired Fedka for that occasion. To impress you, my friend. To give Yevgeny's background that tiny bit of extra weight. *Vanitas vanitatum et omnia vanitas*. Ecclesiastes, I think. But don't trust me on that. I can still quote with some accuracy but the attribution . . . the attribution seems to . . . That lunch, yes. And Fedka. I had asked Father Alexei could he recommend somebody. And what did he present us with? – the butcher's second son with the running nose and not a shoe to his name – in a manner of speaking. Serving at the table, barefoot! Good Lord. I can laugh at it now. I remember I said, 'Arkady Nikolayevich will think he's staying with some sort of primitives.' And Yevgeny lifted his head – you know how he lifts his face and turns it slightly sideways – and gave me that sharp, quick eye of his – and he said – he said – and nobody's wittier than Yevgeny as you well know – he lifted his head and he gave me – gave me— (*He breaks down: Sudden, uncontrollable sobbing. He recovers almost immediately.*)

I should pray to God, they say. How can I go on? – that's what I say to God. How do you expect me to go on? – I say. What do you think we're made of? – I say.

(*Pause.*)

ARKADY: It was very late when I got back from Petersburg. My father was waiting up for me. 'I've got very bad news for you, son. I can't tell you how bad the news is.' 'It's Bazarov,' I said. 'Yes,' he said. 'It's Bazarov.'

(*Pause.*)

VASSILY: At the end of that first week there were so many people sick and dying that we decided to split up: he took the whole town and the region to the north and west. I had the south and east. Some nights he didn't get home at all. And when the epidemic spread to the neighbouring province we didn't see him for days on end. 'All for the bloody peasants,' he said to me. 'Everything for the bloody peasants, damn them!' And then I came in this night – it was Friday – amn't I

76

correct, my pet? There was a light under his bedroom door. And I was tiptoeing past when he called me. He was sitting up in the bed, propped up against the pillow; and even though the candle was behind his head the first thing I noticed was how bright, how bright his eyes shone. And he said in that ironic tone of his, 'Father,' he said, 'I'm going to make you a present of a much larger practice. I'm going to present you with the town and the region to the north and west.' 'What does that mean?' I said. (*His voice begins to waver.*) 'It means,' he said – 'It means,' he said – 'It means that I'm considering retiring. What's your opinion of this, Dr Bazarov? Does it look like typhus?' And he pulled up the sleeve of his night-shirt and held his bare arm over to the candle and there were the purple blotches.

(ARKADY *is now crying quietly.*)

ARKADY: I'm sorry for behaving like this . . .

VASSILY: There was nothing we could do. His mother made him lime-flower tea and she tried to feed him spoonfuls of beetroot and cabbage soup. But he was too weak to swallow anything. And the next morning – that was Sunday – amn't I right, my pet? – yes, I am – that was Sunday – he opened his eyes and said, 'Do something for me, Father. Send a messenger to Anna Sergeyevna Odintsov and tell her that Yevgeny Vassilyich Bazarov is dying.'

ARKADY: All Katya knew was that a messenger came to the house and that within five minutes Anna was gone.

VASSILY: And late that same evening a grey carriage with red wheels and drawn by four horses drew up at our door and a footman in dark green livery opened the carriage door and this lady in a black veil and a black mantle got out. She told me she was Anna Sergeyevna Odintsov and asked to see my son. I argued with her. I said it was too dangerous. But she was determined. So I brought her to him. I left them together. She stayed with him for half an hour. He was too weak to talk. She just sat with him and held his hand.

ARKADY: Nobody has seen her since. She didn't go home when she left here. She sent the carriage home and she went on to Moscow. She probably wants to be by herself for a while.

VASSILY: He passed away that same evening. His mother sent for Father Alexei. He was dead by then but Father Alexei gave him the last rites anyway.

ARKADY: My father didn't know what to do. I was somewhere in the Petersburg area buying a new thresher – that's all he knew. But where I was staying – how to get in touch with me – he was at his wits' end. Finally he sent Piotr to look for me – just to walk the streets of Petersburg and look for me. And all the time I was in our old flat. That never occurred to them.

VASSILY: We tried to get word to some friends. Timofeich did the best he could. I thought it best to have a short wake because of the nature of the illness and because his mother was a little . . . *perturbata*. So we buried him on Monday morning, early. A quiet funeral; his mother, Father Alexei, Timofeich, myself. And Fedka, the worthy Fedka, properly shod. It was nice of him to come. And brave. A few prayers. Flowers. The usual. I'll take you there if you wish. It's only a ten-minute walk. But if you prefer not . . . some people find cemeteries . . . difficult. There's something not right about a father burying his son, isn't there? Some disorder in the proper ordering of things, isn't it? It's not the way things should be, is it?

ARKADY: He was the best friend I ever had, Vassily Ivanyich. (*Pause.*)

VASSILY: (*Almost in a whisper but with a sudden and astonishing passion*) Damn you, Almighty Father! I will not stand for it! I certainly will not stand for it!

ARKADY: He was the only real friend I ever had.

VASSILY: What's that?

ARKADY: (*Suddenly resolute*) I'm going to carry on his work, Vassily Ivanyich! I'm going to dedicate myself to his memory and to the work he was so involved in! I have none of his brains and none of his talent. But whatever talent I have and whatever energy I have I will give to the revolution, to Bazarov's revolution.

VASSILY: (*Dreamily*) Oh, yes. Politics are very important.

ARKADY: He never thought I was capable of much. But I am! I

am! And I am now more than ever because I'm doing it for him!

(VASSILY *pats him on the shoulder*.)

VASSILY: Every so often he would regain consciousness. One time he opened his eyes and he said, 'I am no loss to Russia. A cobbler would be a loss to Russia. A butcher would be a loss. A tailor would be a loss. I am no loss.' It never occurred to him the loss he'd be to his mother and me.

ARKADY: If you would take me to the cemetery, I'd like to make my solemn promise to him there.

(ARINA *enters, her hair dishevelled, wearing slippers and an odd assortment of clothes. When she enters her face is vacant. Then she sees* VASSILY *and she smiles.* VASSILY *greets her with great warmth and enthusiasm.* ARKADY *gets to his feet.*)

VASSILY: Ah – Arina! Now that's an improvement! Now you're looking really well, my pet! Do you know that you slept for almost three hours? And who's going to do the housework if my wife lies in bed and spends the day sleeping? Tell me that, my sweet and beautiful wife? And look who's here! Look who's come to see us!

(*She looks blankly at* ARKADY.)

Yes! It's Arkady, my pet! It is, indeed! Arkady Nikolayevich! The very moment he heard he came straight over. He was afraid he'd have to leave without seeing you.

ARKADY: All I can say, Arina Vlasseyevna – (*He begins to cry again*.) – all I can say is that – that – that – that I'm shattered, just shattered.

VASSILY: We've looked after ourselves as you can see. But what we've got to do now is get you something to eat. What can I offer you? What would tempt you? I have it! Arina Vlassyevna is partial to a cup of blackcurrant tea! The very thing!

ARKADY: I'll never forgive myself that I wasn't here. I was away in Petersburg. I didn't hear a thing until late last night.

VASSILY: (*Breezy, busy*) One small cup of blackcurrant tea and two very tiny but very appetizing home-made biscuits – that's what this aristocratic lady requires and that is what she is going to eat. What does Cicero say? *Tantum cibi et potionis*

     – we should drink and eat just enough to restore our
     strength – no more, no less.

ARKADY: I can't tell you how devastated I am. I know I'll never
     get over it.

     (ARINA *now sits. Pause. She looks at* ARKADY *as if she were
     trying to remember him, as if she were going to speak to him. Her
     face is placid, child-like, almost smiling. And when she sings it is
     the gentle, high-pitched voice of a very young girl.*)

ARINA: (*Sings*) *Te Deum laudamus: te Dominum confitemur. Te
     aeternum Patrem omnis terra veneratur.*

     (*As soon as she begins singing* ARKADY *looks in alarm at
     *VASSILY. VASSILY *responds by putting his finger to his lips and
     shaking his head as if to say – Say nothing; don't interrupt. Then
     he sits beside his wife, puts both arms round her, and sings with
     her and directly to her*:

VASSILY } *Tibi omnes Angeli, tibi Caeli et universae Potestates.*
ARINA } *Tibi Cherubim et Seraphim incessabili voce proclament:*
       Sanctus, Sanctus, Sanctus, Dominus Deus Sabaoth.
       (*Slowly bring down the lights as they sing together.*)

*After dinner. Early October. The lawn-garden in front of the
Kirsanov home.*

ARKADY *is standing at the piano and singing 'Drink to me only'. He
sight-reads the words.* KATYA *accompanies him.* ANNA *sits by herself
in the living-room, listening to the music.*

PAVEL *stands on the veranda.*

PAVEL: (*Sings very softly*)

> 'But might I of Jove's nectar sup,
> I would not change for thine.'

FENICHKA: Very nice, Pavel.

> (PAVEL *realizing that he has been overheard wags his finger
> in admonition. He then lapses into his own private thoughts.
> Two or three times we hear the faint sound of dance music played
> on the piano-accordion some distance away. These brief
> coincidences of the two sounds – the piano and the piano-
> accordion – produce an almost eerie noise.*
>
> *The* PRINCESS *is sitting alone downstage right, partly concealed
> behind her unnecessary parasol, vigorously masticating and every
> so often brushing her sleeve and skirt.*
>
> PROKOFYICH *and* PIOTR *have assembled a large trestle-table
> in the centre of the lawn. They now cover it with a white cloth
> and arrange chairs around it.*
>
> FENICHKA *oversees this work with a proprietorial eye. She is
> now very much mistress of the house and fully at ease in* PAVEL's
> *presence.* PIOTR, *slightly intoxicated, is completely restored to
> health and cockiness and jaunty self-assurance. He nips down
> behind the gazebo on the pretext of getting a chair and tosses back
> a quick, secret drink from a hip-flask. He is about to pour a
> second drink when the* PRINCESS *calls him.*)

PRINCESS: You, boy! Come here! Come here! Come here!

> (*He quickly hides his flask and does a little dance as he goes to
> her.*)

PIOTR: Princess, can I help you?

PRINCESS: What's that noise?

PIOTR: That noise, Princess, is Arkady singing and Miss Katya playing the piano for—

PRINCESS: The noise! The damn noise! There – d'you hear that?

PIOTR: My apologies. That is the musician getting ready for tonight – the annual harvest dance. We hold it in the granary.

PRINCESS: Musician? What musician?

PIOTR: A piano-accordion player, Princess. He comes from the town of Orel.

PRINCESS: My brother, Josef, had the first accordion ever brought into Russia. My father lit a bonfire in the yard and burned the damn thing before the whole household. Then he whipped Josef with his own hunting crop until he apologized publicly to everybody – family and servants. Ha-ha. That ended damn accordions in our house!

PIOTR: I'm sure it did.

PRINCESS: Josef was black and blue for a month. Tell your friend from Orel that story. Ha-ha. Whipped him! Whipped him! Whipped him!

PIOTR: I'll tell him, Princess.

(*She withdraws.* PIOTR *returns to his work.* PAVEL *comes down and joins* FENICHKA.)

PAVEL: I bought that song-book in London – oh, it must be twenty-five years ago. (*Suddenly remembering.*) I know exactly when I bought it – the day they made Arthur Wellesley foreign secretary. We were out on the town, celebrating!

FENICHKA: Who was that, Pavel?

PAVEL: Arthur? The first Duke of Wellington. Good man. Good fun. We had a lot of laughs together . . .
Nice time of the day, this.

FENICHKA: Lovely.

PAVEL: Nice time of the year. Do you like October, Olga?

PRINCESS: I detest every month – for different reasons.

PAVEL: It's my favourite season, the autumn. I tell myself it's the one time of the year when the environment and my nature are perfectly attuned.

PRINCESS: It seems to me you tell yourself a lot of rubbish. And

82

you'd need to be careful – the way you carry yourself – you
could be mistaken for an accordion player.

PAVEL: I beg your pardon?

PRINCESS: You look very like one to me, with your shoulders so
far back.

PAVEL: (*To* FENICHKA) I didn't catch what she said. I could
be a – ?

FENICHKA: An accordion player.

PAVEL: Me?!

PRINCESS: They all carry their shoulders back. That's because
the weight is all down the front here. Ha-ha, you could end
up being whipped by mistake!

PAVEL: Good heavens, could I? (*To* FENICHKA.) Why do they
whip accordion players?

FENICHKA: I don't know. Do they?

PAVEL: So it seems.

FENICHKA: (*To* PIOTR) There's a vase of dahlias and a vase of
chrysanthemums outside the pantry door. Put the dahlias
here and the chrysanthemums there.

PIOTR: Anything the lady wishes.

PAVEL: Arkady has a pleasing voice. From the mother's side of
the house. Maria had a sweet voice.

FENICHKA: (*To* PIOTR *as he dances off*) And napkins from the
linen-press. On the top shelf. (*To* PAVEL) What is that song?

PAVEL: 'Drink to me only'.

FENICHKA: I never heard him singing that before.

PAVEL: (*Speaks*)
  'I sent thee late a rosy wreath,
  Not so much honouring thee
  As giving it a hope that there
  It could not withered be . . .'

(FENICHKA *has been counting the chairs*.)

FENICHKA: Sorry, Pavel – what was that?

PAVEL: Nothing. Just mumbling to myself.

(DUNYASHA *enters left*.)

FENICHKA: I've noticed you doing that a lot recently. You're not
beginning to dote, are you? There are only wine glasses here,
Dunyasha. Bring out the champagne glasses, will you?

(PAVEL, *wounded, moves away.* DUNYASHA *is so excited she can scarcely keep her voice down.* FENICHKA *continues moving around the table, adjusting the settings.* DUNYASHA *follows her.* FENICHKA *listens with interest but her manner hints that the days of confidences are over.*)

DUNYASHA: Brilliant news, Fenichka! Absolutely brilliant! The aunt died at half past three this morning! Can you believe it!

FENICHKA: Who?

DUNYASHA: The aunt – the old aunt – the old bitch that reared Adam!

FENICHKA: Oh, I'm sorry to hear—

DUNYASHA: He'll be able to sell her cottage. And she has left him about two hundred roubles. And he wants to get married, Fenichka!

FENICHKA: To you?

DUNYASHA: Jesus, you don't think he fancies the Tailor's Dummy, do you?!

FENICHKA: Dunyasha, I—

DUNYASHA: Of course it's to me! At five this morning – the old cow couldn't have been right stiff – he was up banging on my bedroom door: 'Little one, will you make me the happiest man in Russia?' That's what he said! Can a duck swim, says I to myself. He didn't go back to the corp-house till well after nine. Jesus, you should have seen that glossy black 'tash of his twitching! D'you know what we should do, Fenichka? – you hang on for another couple of months and we'll get married together! Wouldn't that be a howl! A double wedding! Drive the poor old Tailor's Dummy astray in the head altogether!

FENICHKA: I don't want you to call Pavel Petrovich by that name again, Dunyasha.

DUNYASHA: The Tailor's Dummy? Between ourselves, for God's sake; it's only to you and Piotr and—

FENICHKA: I never want to hear it again.

DUNYASHA: Are you – ?

FENICHKA: Is that clearly understood? Good. I'm sorry about the old aunt. But Adam should have no regrets: he was more

84

than attentive to her. I'll take those napkins from you, Piotr; thank you. You arranged those flowers beautifully, Dunyasha. I'm glad you're thinking of marrying him. He'll make a very reliable husband. Now – what's missing? The champagne glasses. (*To* DUNYASHA.) Would you get them for me?

(DUNYASHA *stumps off.*)

No, the other way round, Piotr – the dahlias on this side. Don't you think so?

PIOTR: I'm sure you're right. The dahlias are left-handed. (*While he was out* PIOTR *has had a few more drinks.*) What else can I do for you, Fenichka? You just tell Piotr.

FENICHKA: That's all for now.

PIOTR: Have you enough chairs?

FENICHKA: I think so.

PIOTR: What about some stools?

FENICHKA: They won't be needed.

PIOTR: Stools are a very efficient means of seating large numbers of guests in an outdoor environment, Fenichka.

FENICHKA: We haven't got large numbers, Piotr.

PIOTR: Once again you are right. Another few bottles of wine, perhaps?

FENICHKA: (*Dismissing him*) Thank you, Piotr.

PIOTR: I know a poem. Would you like me to recite it?

FENICHKA: Not now, Piotr.

PIOTR: Later perhaps. I could spell chrysanthemum for you.

FENICHKA: That is all for the time being, Piotr.

PIOTR: Well, as soon as the time being is up, Piotr will be at your elbow and at your command.

(*He bows formally and goes off left.*)

FENICHKA: The harvest party has begun early. (*She holds up an empty bottle.*) Since lunch time.

(*To* ANNA *who comes out.*)

Come and join us, Anna.

ANNA: The days are shortening already, aren't they?

(*She pauses beside the* PRINCESS.)

Are you all right, Auntie?

PRINCESS: Why do you always ask that absurd question when

you know the answer. No, I am not all right. There's a constant buzzing in my head. I can scarcely walk with arthritis. That meal they gave us was inedible. And I am about to be sick with the smell of cat in this damn place. (*She rises and leaves left.*) When you're ready to leave you'll find me in the paddock. There's a black filly there that needs to be broken.

ANNA: She gets great comfort from her misery.

PAVEL: I'm studying her carefully. We could have a lot in common.

FENICHKA: You don't have her vigour, Pavel.

PAVEL: I could simulate that, too, couldn't I?

FENICHKA: Nikolai tells me you had a good harvest.

ANNA: I was away for most of it. Yes, it was a good harvest. (*She gestures her indifference.*) The best I've ever had . . . It's good to hear Arkady singing.

FENICHKA: Yes.

ANNA: And Katerina tells me he's out and about again.

FENICHKA: He hadn't much choice. The estate's his now. He was needed on the land.

ANNA: They're a handsome couple.

PAVEL: Aren't they.

ANNA: A pity you'll miss the wedding, Pavel.

FENICHKA: The weddings, Anna.

ANNA: Of course.

PAVEL: Yes, I'm sorry about that. I'm due to arrive in Zurich that day.

(FENICHKA *waters the plants in front of the veranda.*)

Any news of the epidemic? – the typhus epidemic?

ANNA: I'm told it's almost died out.

PAVEL: Has it?

ANNA: So I've heard.

PAVEL: Ah. Good.

ANNA: Yes.

PAVEL: So it's over now?

ANNA: Almost. Not quite.

PAVEL: Good. They cause great devastation, those things. But they pass – they pass.

ANNA: That's true.

PAVEL: And the world carries on.

ANNA: I suppose so. Yes, of course it does.
(*Pause.*)

PAVEL: I got to know him slightly just before he left here. I hadn't understood him at all before that. In my stupidity. He was a fine man.

ANNA: He was also a . . . difficult man.

PAVEL: He was that, too.

ANNA: He wanted to marry me.

PAVEL: I gathered that.

ANNA: (*Crying quietly*) I should have married him, Pavel . . .

PAVEL: Perhaps – perhaps.

ANNA: Oh, yes, I should. Oh, yes. It would have been a difficult marriage but I should have married him. It's very hard to carry on when you know you've made so enormous a mistake, Pavel. How do you carry on?

PAVEL: I wish I could help you, Anna. I very much wish I could help you. I have no answers to anything. We all want to believe at least in the possibility of one great love. And when we cannot achieve it – because it isn't achievable – we waste our lives pursuing surrogates; at least those of us who are very foolish do.

FENICHKA: Soon be time to bring them inside.

PAVEL: And that's no life, no life at all.
(*He puts his hands on* ANNA'*s shoulders.*)
A kind of contentment is available, Anna: in routine, acceptance, duty.

ANNA: I had that life.

PAVEL: It has its consolations. Is that a terrible thing to say?

ANNA: He thought so.

PAVEL: I know. But it's the only threadbare wisdom I have for you. I don't believe a word of it myself.
(DUNYASHA *enters with the glasses. She barely conceals her fury.*)

DUNYASHA: Miss, the champagne glasses, miss.

FENICHKA: (*Very calm*) Thank you, Dunyasha. Put them on the table.

DUNYASHA: Is there anything else I can get you, miss?

FENICHKA: That will be all for now, Dunyasha.

DUNYASHA: Sir, what about you, sir?

PAVEL: Sorry?

DUNYASHA: Sir, can I get you anything, sir?

PAVEL: (*Alarmed at this attention*) Me? No . . . nothing . . . nothing, thank you.

(DUNYASHA *stumps off into the house.*

NIKOLAI *enters from the left. He is wearing a very brightly coloured jacket – a jacket for a much younger man.*

Now and again bring up the sound of distant piano-accordion music.)

NIKOLAI: I've held you all up, have I?

FENICHKA: I thought you'd gone dancing by yourself.

NIKOLAI: Ha-ha. Just saying a word of formal thanks and encouragement to the workers for their sterling efforts over the past weeks.

(*Quick kiss and embrace for* FENICHKA.)

This looks splendid! Excellent! I love those dahlias.

FENICHKA: These are the dahlias.

NIKOLAI: Are they? I never get them right. They're beautiful anyhow. (*To all*) Incidentally some time later on it would be greatly appreciated if we all put in a brief appearance at the dance; just to – you know – just to – to pass ourselves. No obligation whatever to – to participate – not that some of us could – (*Indicates his lameness.*) – even if we wished to. I'll ask Arkady to dance with you on my behalf – just once!

PAVEL: You'll have to let me have one dance, too, Nikolai.

NIKOLAI: Yes?

PAVEL: Of course. The brother-in-law to be. I was an excellent dancer once upon a time. (*To* FENICHKA.) That's agreed, then.

NIKOLAI: Good. Good. Yes. Fine. Anyhow. Now to organize our lives. Is everybody here?

(*He looks into the living-room where* KATYA *and* ARKADY *are talking heatedly.*)

Look at those two love-birds.

(KATYA *bangs the piano-lid shut.*)

FENICHKA: Squabbling love-birds.

NIKOLAI: Arkady! Katya! Come out here at once! Where's the Princess?

ANNA: She's walking around somewhere.

NIKOLAI: I'll go and get her.

ANNA: No. Leave her. She's happier by herself.

(KATYA *and* ARKADY *join the others.*)

ARKADY: Well – well – well – well! (*Ironic clapping.*) Feast your eyes on that wonderful sight!

NIKOLAI: What's the matter?

ARKADY: Just look at that astonishing jacket! Where did that come from?

NIKOLAI: I agree with you, Arkady. I think myself it's much too young for a man of—

FENICHKA: I chose it, Arkady.

ARKADY: Did you now?

FENICHKA: And I think he's very handsome in it.

KATYA: So he is. And it's a wonderful jacket. (*To* ARKADY.) We all agree.

ARKADY: I'm sure you do. I still think it's remarkable.

(NIKOLAI *does a mock pirouette.*)

NIKOLAI: What do you think, Anna?

ANNA: (*In a reverie*) Sorry – sorry?

NIKOLAI: Do you approve of it?

ANNA: Approve of – ?

PAVEL: (*Quickly*) We all think you're gorgeous, Nikolai. And I'm madly jealous. One Tailor's Dummy in the house is sufficient.

NIKOLAI: Who is the Tailor's Dummy?

PAVEL: Didn't you know? That's what the servants call me.

NIKOLAI: I never heard that, Pavel.

PAVEL: I don't mind in the least. It's not without affection, is it?

FENICHKA: Show them the lining, Nikolai.

NIKOLAI: I certainly will not!

FENICHKA: Go on! For my sake.

(*With mock coyness* NIKOLAI *unbuttons the jacket and opens it to reveal an even more brilliant lining.*
Applause and laughter.)

NIKOLAI: And this, of course, is the real Nikolai Petrovich.

FENICHKA: Feast your eyes on that!

KATYA: Yes – yes – yes – yes!

ARKADY: Ridiculous.

FENICHKA: And when he's tired of it, I'm going to wear it – inside out.

NIKOLAI: Enough of this. I'm not sure you're all not taking a hand at me. Let's all gather round the table and get a glass. There's going to be no formality. And no speeches. Just an exchange of congratulations and good wishes between friends. Come over here beside me, Fenichka. Has everybody got something in his glass?

KATYA: (*Filling her glass*) Just a second, Nikolai.

NIKOLAI: Give me your hand, Katya. Good. Splendid. Well. The harvest is saved. It has been a good, an especially good, year. And first of all we want to thank you most warmly, Anna – don't we, Arkady? – most warmly indeed for all the tremendous help you have been to us not only in your advice and wisdom over the past months but more particularly, indeed most particularly, for your spontaneous and generous offer of your machinery – an offer, may I say—

ARKADY: You said no speeches.

NIKOLAI: And there'll be none.

ARKADY: Good. Thank you, Anna.

NIKOLAI: Thank you most sincerely, Anna. And if the situation is ever—

ARKADY: Father!

NIKOLAI: Sorry – sorry. Thank you. We all thank Anna – don't we?

(*Clapping. Raising of glasses.*)

FENICHKA: Incidentally did you hear that Adam's old aunt has died?

NIKOLAI: Somebody did mention that. When did it happen?

FENICHKA: Early this morning. Are you still thinking of sacking him?

NIKOLAI: Yes. No. He worked like a Trojan this past month. But this is a matter for you, Arkady. You're master of the estate now.

ARKADY: I'll think about it. I'll watch him. He knows he's on
    probation.
NIKOLAI: Why do you ask?
FENICHKA: No reason. Just wondering. Who's for more wine?
KATYA: Me, please. We're all going to miss you very much,
    Uncle Pavel.
PAVEL: For all of two minutes.
ARKADY: I think you've had enough wine, Katya.
KATYA: (*Dismissively*) I'll make that decision. (*To* PAVEL.) Yes,
    we will. A whole lot.
PAVEL: (*To* KATYA) Did I hear you playing 'Drink to me only'?
KATYA: And Arkady was singing. Weren't you?
    (ARKADY *ignores her*.)
NIKOLAI: That used to be my song . . . long ago . . .
    Shakespeare wrote the words – did you know that?
PAVEL: No.
NIKOLAI: Yes, he did.
PAVEL: Jonson.
NIKOLAI: What's that, Pavel?
PAVEL: A contemporary of Shakespeare.
NIKOLAI: Yes?
PAVEL: Ben Jonson.
NIKOLAI: What about him?
PAVEL: He wrote the words.
NIKOLAI: What words?
PAVEL: Ben Jonson.
NIKOLAI: Who is this Ben Jonson, Pavel?
PAVEL: Nothing – nothing – just that you said that Shakespeare
    wrote the words of—
ARKADY: (*Shouts*) Who cares! (*Controlled*.) Who cares who wrote
    the bloody words! Who gives a damn! Exactly four weeks
    ago today Bazarov died – and who cares about that? – Who
    even remembers? Not even one of you! All you care about is
    stupid jackets and big harvests and stupid bloody songs!
    Well, I care. And I remember. And I will always remember.
    And in the coming years I'm going to devote my life to his
    beliefs and his philosophy – to our philosophy – to carrying
    out his revolution. That's what I'm going to do for the rest of

my life. And nothing in the world – absolutely nothing – is going to stop me!

(*He breaks down and cries.*

There is a long, embarrassed silence. KATYA *pours another drink.* NIKOLAI, *unable to endure the silence, begins to hum but tails off quickly. Silence again.*

Then FENICHKA *goes to* NIKOLAI *and whispers in his ear.*)

NIKOLAI: Sorry? What's that?

FENICHKA: The books.

NIKOLAI: Books? What books? Oh the books! Of course! Piotr'll get them for me. P—

(*He is about to shout 'Piotr!' – and miraculously there is* PIOTR, *now very drunk, at his elbow.*)

Ah. There you are, Piotr. Isn't that remarkable?

PIOTR: Sir.

NIKOLAI: I didn't call you, did I?

PIOTR: Yes, sir, you did.

NIKOLAI: Did I?

PIOTR: With great clarity. Twice. And here I am.

NIKOLAI: Well, if you say so, Piotr. Splendid. Run up to my bedroom and on the table beside my bed you'll find two books. Bring them here to me, will you?

(*Pause.*)

PIOTR: C-h-r-y-s-

NIKOLAI: Sorry? What's that?

PIOTR: C-h-r-y-s-a-n-t-

NIKOLAI: What's he saying?

PIOTR: -r-y-s-a-n-t-m-t-m-r-s-y-

(*The others laugh.* PROKOFYICH, *stiff and stern, enters.*)

NIKOLAI: You're not intoxicated, Piotr, are you?

PIOTR: I know it. I'm telling you I know it. Let me try again. C-h-r-s-y-

(PROKOFYICH *leads* PIOTR *off left.*)

PROKOFYICH: Come on, boy. You're for bed. (*To all.*) Sorry about this. It won't happen again. Come on. Move, boy. (*To all.*) You know you are all cordially invited to the dance later on.

NIKOLAI: Thank you, Prokofyich. We'll go for a short time.

PROKOFYICH: Very good. I'm sorry about this.

(*They exit;* PIOTR *still trying to spell.*)

KATYA: I'll get those books, Nikolai.

NIKOLAI: Poor old Piotr. Poor boy must be suffering terribly.

FENICHKA: He's been at it since lunch-time.

PAVEL: And it's time I went and got some packing done. I hope
the wedding – No weddings – will be a great success. I'm
sure they will. (*Produces a tiny box.*) I have ordered a proper
present – it's due to arrive at the end of the week. In the
meantime – it's only a token.

(*He hands the box to* FENICHKA.)

FENICHKA: Thank you very much, Pavel.

NIKOLAI: What is this?

FENICHKA: It's a ring. It's beautiful, Pavel, really beautiful.
Thank you.

NIKOLAI: Let me see.

(FENICHKA *kisses* PAVEL *on the cheek.*)

PAVEL: Make it two dances.

NIKOLAI: Lovely, Pavel. Thank you very much. What's
engraved on the stone? Is it a sphinx?

PAVEL: Is it? It's only a token. No value whatever.

FENICHKA: I don't believe that.

NIKOLAI: Put it on.

FENICHKA: I love it. I'll think of you every time I wear it.

NIKOLAI: It's a beautiful memento, Pavel.

PAVEL: *Magnifique!* That's two occasions I'll be recalled:
whenever you wear that ring; and every time borzoi fanciers
get together and Katya's damned pup is discussed. (*To*
ARKADY.) I've ordered something for you and Katya, too. I
hope you'll like it.

ARKADY: Thank you – from both of us.

(KATYA *returns with two books.*)

KATYA: Here you are.

NIKOLAI: Thank you, Katya. And these are for you, Pavel.
Something to read on your journeyings.

PAVEL: What's this?

NIKOLAI: Fenichka chose them. We hope you like them.

PAVEL: Mrs Ann Ward Radcliffe! Never! *The Romance of the*

Forest and *The Mysteries of Udolpho*. Wonderful! Where did you get them? They've been out of print for years!

FENICHKA: Piotr hunted them out when he was in Petersburg last month.

PAVEL: Absolutely wonderful! You couldn't have given me greater pleasure! Darling, innocent Mrs Ann Ward Radcliffe. And the two I'm missing. Can I bear so much intellectual stimulation?

(*General laughter. He kisses* FENICHKA *and then* NIKOLAI.)

NIKOLAI: Brother – brother Pavel.

PAVEL: I'll carry them with me wherever I go. *Merci. Merci beaucoup*.

NIKOLAI: (*Wiping away his tears*) Now. One final toast. Yes, I'm sorry, Arkady. I'm going to make a short speech – a very short speech.

KATYA: I would like to hear a very long speech.

NIKOLAI: What I just want to say is that this house, this home, is about to suffer a permanent and irreparable loss. Pavel is leaving. We will miss him terribly. And I want him to know that wherever he goes, our love will accompany him always, everywhere. But there is a silver lining to – to – to every— We do have a compensation, indeed a very substantial compensation. Fenichka Fedosya has consented to be my wife and for that – that – that benediction I am profoundly grateful. And on the same day – this day two weeks, amn't I correct? – and on this very lawn another marriage will be celebrated between Katya Sergeyevna and my son, Arkady. And by that union, too, I am profoundly gratified. Some people might think that there is something inappropriate about a father and a son getting married on the same day, some disorder in the proper ordering of things. But I know that for both of us it will be an occasion of great joy and great fulfilment. And who is to determine what is the proper ordering of things?

(*Bring up the accordion playing 'Drink to me only'*.)

FENICHKA: Listen, Nikolai.

NIKOLAI: (*To* KATYA) That clever musician – he picked it up from you.

94

(*They all listen for a few seconds.*)
That was our song, long, long ago. Maria and I. I sang the
melody and she sang the seconds. Our party piece. Her
eyelids fluttered when she sang. Shakespeare wrote the
words – did you know that?
(*He begins to sing.* FENICHKA *watches him with a strained
smile. He puts his arm around her and hugs her.*)
Sing!
(*She gives him an uncertain smile but does not sing.*
KATYA *moves beside* ARKADY. *She catches his hand. She
begins to sing and sings the words directly into his face. He does
not sing.*
PAVEL *moves across to* ANNA *who is sitting away from the
others. He catches her hand.*)
PAVEL: Do you sing?
ANNA: Occasionally. When I'm alone.
PAVEL: Yes. *Je comprends* . . .
NIKOLAI: ⎫
KATYA: ⎭

> Drink to me only with thine eyes,
> And I will pledge with mine;
> Or leave a kiss but in the cup
> And I'll not look for wine.
> The thirst that from the soul doth rise
> Doth ask a drink divine;
> But might I of Jove's nectar sup,
> I would not change for thine.